POLITICS, POVERTY AND BELIEF: A POLITICAL MEMOIR

POLITICS, POVERTY AND BELIEF: A POLITICAL MEMOIR

Frank Field

BLOOMSBURY CONTINUUM
LONDON · OXFORD · NEW YORK · NEW DELHI · SYDNEY

BLOOMSBURY CONTINUUM
Bloomsbury Publishing Plc
50 Bedford Square, London, WC1B 3DP, UK
29 Earlsfort Terrace, Dublin 2, Ireland

BLOOMSBURY, BLOOMSBURY CONTINUUM and the Diana logo are trademarks
of Bloomsbury Publishing Plc

First published in Great Britain 2023

A catalogue record for this book is available from the British Library

Library of Congress Cataloguing-in-Publication data has been applied for

ISBN: HB: 978-1-3994-0839-4; eBook: 978-1-3994-0840-0; ePDF: 978-1-3994-0843-1

2 4 6 8 10 9 7 5 3

Typeset by Deanta Global Publishing Services, Chennai, India
Printed and bound in Great Britain by CPI Group (UK) Ltd, Croydon CR0 4YY

MIX
Paper | Supporting
responsible forestry
FSC® C171272

To find out more about our authors and books visit www.bloomsbury.com
and sign up for our newsletters

CONTENTS

Introduction

Frank Field on Faith and Politics

by Brian and Rachel Griffiths

For the past half-century Frank Field has been an outstanding parliamentarian, social reformer and champion of the disadvantaged. He joined the Labour Party at the age of 16 and was expelled from it at the age of 78, after he withdrew from the party whip over the failure of the party's National Executive to investigate bullying and intimidation by Momentum in the Birkenhead Labour Party. He was MP for Birkenhead for four decades, a Minister for Welfare Reform in Tony Blair's first government and chair of three select committees of the House of Commons. Before he entered Parliament, and throughout his time as an MP, he campaigned on a wide range of issues, including child poverty, low pay, council house sales, modern-day slavery, hunger and climate change, and was invariably knowledgeable, articulate and a gifted communicator.

By the public he was generally seen as a model member of the House of Commons: totally committed to his constituents, hard-working, with a modest lifestyle, total integrity and not a whiff of scandal or conflict of interest,

1

and committed to fighting for social justice, greater equality and the common good of society. To spend a day with Frank, not just in the north-west but in any part of the UK, meant being constantly interrupted by members of the public, of all shades of political opinion, thanking him for what he had done and for who he was.

After he was defeated in Birkenhead he was given a peerage as Lord Field of Birkenhead and in 2022 was made a Companion of Honour by Queen Elizabeth.

However, by colleagues he was often seen as an enigma: awkward, unreliable and to some extent a troublemaker. He was not afraid to speak his mind and was a nightmare for party whips. Ruth Runciman once remonstrated with Tony Blair for not having Frank in the Shadow Cabinet, to which Blair replied, 'He can be a bit awkward, you know.' She in turn replied, 'Tony, being awkward is the point of Frank.'

That Frank was 'a bit awkward' was already evident before he became an MP. During his term as Director, the Child Poverty Action Group (CPAG) published *The Poor Get Poorer under Labour* in the year before the Conservative victory at the 1970 general election. It was the product of meticulous research conducted with Professor Peter Townsend. Frank was well aware that the title of the memorandum would not endear him to the Labour leadership, and he was right. Richard (Dick) Crossman, who was Secretary of State for Health and Social Security at the time, and his influential adviser Professor Brian

Abel-Smith were both furious and wanted to prevent publication of the pamphlet. Crossman invited Frank and Peter Townsend to meet him at the Cabinet Office. There was a long, polished table in the room. Crossman and Abel-Smith sat at one end, Frank and Peter Townsend at the other, and they debated the findings. As the meeting ended, Crossman, furious and frustrated, said, 'Well, if this is published, no one will ever believe you,' to which Frank replied, 'Then you don't need to worry about it, do you?'

Frank always claimed that he was 'never in any box from which he had to escape but always on the outside'. He campaigned for the poor, the disadvantaged and the low-paid, yet he believed in the market economy because it generated jobs and prosperity and could bring new opportunities, such as a free port to Birkenhead. He was committed to the Labour Party and yet had great respect for Margaret Thatcher and was one of the last people to see her in No. 10 on the night before she resigned as Prime Minister.

We came across Frank Field's work in the early 1970s, not long after we had ourselves moved across the political spectrum from left to right. The more we read of his publications and press releases, the more we kept asking ourselves, 'Who is this Frank Field?' When Brian was head of the Prime Minister's Policy Unit he met Frank in person when he came into No. 10 along with Lord Pilkington to lobby for increased parental choice in schools, different kinds of schools and greater resources devoted to secondary technical education. He was engaging, well informed and knew exactly what he wanted. We did not know at the time the strength of his Christian faith, but this meeting started a friendship which has grown ever since.

Frank Field began writing *Politics, Poverty and Belief* in 2010. He wanted to show that his political views and campaigns were derived from and inextricably interwoven with his Christian faith. Living at a time when the Christian faith was in dramatic decline, he recognized that much of his speaking and writing had been to a secular audience, and that in it he had deliberately avoided religious language or Church affiliation. He feared that he might be perceived as a secularist and wanted to make it clear that his political views and actions were founded on the moral values and virtues that derived from his Christian faith. He believed that we could no more invent these fundamental values by human reason alone than that we could invent new primary colours or decide to dispense with the law of gravity. But he also felt that, in public life today, to mention one's Christian faith risked being thought of as a bit of a crank or, at the very least, as someone who had abandoned their critical faculties.

We have discussed the contents of the book with him on many occasions in London and Wales and through many drafts. When he was told that he had possibly only weeks to live, he felt he would never finish the book and asked if we would 'complete it'. The text of the book is entirely his. However, as those weeks became months we discussed the text in great detail. When coming to our home or meeting in Parliament became too tiring for him, we met in his flat. Over the last summer, when we were in Wales and he was in London, we had long telephone calls, when we discussed countless questions raised by the existing draft. He was quite weak by this time, but his voice would get stronger as we talked. He was still very concerned about everything that was going on in the political world and in the battles he had fought. His mind was very clear, his memory for details of the past remarkable and his spirits invariably buoyed up by a discussion of the text.

Frank and Brian came from similar social and economic backgrounds but different political environments. Frank's suburban London family were solidly Tory, whereas at the western end of the South Wales coal and steel belt in which Brian was raised it was said that even the air was red with socialism. Both diverged from their political roots and in so doing probably disappointed their parents to some extent. It might seem odd that we should have struck up a friendship. In the 1970s Frank was lobbying for increased welfare benefits while Brian was an academic economist at the London School of Economics (LSE), advocating cutting public expenditure as a way of bringing inflation under control. In the 1980s Frank was a member of the Labour Party committed to redistribution of income and wealth, whereas Brian worked for Margaret Thatcher, committed to privatization, deregulation and enterprise in order to increase jobs, income and wealth, and took the Conservative whip when he entered the House of Lords.

We also came from very different Christian traditions, Frank devoted to the Church of England and from an Anglo-Catholic background, Brian from an Evangelical low church tradition. Frank's reading in theology was almost entirely confined to Anglican writers, whereas Brian's was originally in the Reformed Calvinist tradition of social and political thinkers such as Jean Calvin, Abraham Kuyper and Herman Dooyeweerd, and then later through the encouragement of Michael Novak's Catholic Social Teaching. Although liturgically an Anglo-Catholic, Frank read little of Catholic Social Teaching, which always surprised Brian, as did the fact that he did not involve himself in debate with Christians on the left such as Raymond Plant, John Milbank, Richard Harries, David Sheppard or Malcolm Brown. Despite our differences, these conversations got to the very roots of our shared faith in Jesus Christ, and not only clarified Frank's views but were also a challenge and inspiration to us.

Instead of writing a preface, Frank has asked us to write an introductory essay to the book, which he said was to be his 'death mask', the vision of himself through which he wanted future generations to remember him. The reason he chose us is that he claimed that we probably understood his views on the relationship between his Christian faith and politics better than anyone else.

The earliest and lasting influence of faith on his politics derived from being brought up in a Christian family. He saw his mother as an example of 'living the Kingdom'. The parish church to which she took him, St Nicholas, Chiswick, formed his faith and gave him a love for a tradition of worship which he would term low-church Catholic, and from which he never departed. St Nicholas gave him a sense of belonging to a community greater than the family and a place where he felt totally accepted and at home. It was the Church of England, the national established church, of which the monarch is the Supreme Governor. One of the clues to understanding Frank is his Englishness, and nowhere is this clearer than in his attachment to the Church of England.

As Frank grew up, St Nicholas's provided him with a sacramental perspective, in which everything in the world was imbued with metaphysical meaning. The procession before Mass, in which he took part as an altar boy, was for him literally a movement from the darkness of the vestry to the light of the sanctuary, a vivid image of the Christian journey and something that has remained with him through life. It was from St Nicholas that he learned that God is a mystery and not the exclusive grasp of any one particular theology or philosophy. The fact that Anglicanism was able to hold together differing patterns of worship and understanding was for Frank one its great strengths. St Nicholas's also gave him a sense of Providence, a feeling of being protected by God that remained with him throughout his life.

What St Nicholas's did not provide, however, was 'a scaffolding of ideas', 'a map and a compass', a 'philosophy of life' that would enable him to relate his faith to the worlds of ideas, philosophy and politics. When he went to study economics and politics at the University of Hull, Frank found the gap between a sacramental faith and practical politics a problem. One person at Hull who had a lasting influence on him was John Saville (born Orestis Stamatopoulos), a Marxist historian and professor of economic history. Saville had left the Communist Party Historians' Group following the Soviet invasion of Hungary in 1956.

Another influential figure was A. H. Birch, the Professor of Political Studies at Hull, who introduced him to the concepts of representative and responsible government as the two ideas underpinning British democracy.

Despite having studied politics and political thought as an undergraduate, the driving force of Frank's political interest was not in the realm of ideas or philosophy but in tackling practical problems of injustice. It was revulsion with apartheid in South Africa which led him to join the Labour Party. It was the scale of poverty in the 1960s and '70s, not just of children but those on low pay, unemployed and with inadequate pensions, which led him to apply for the post of Director of the Child Poverty Action Group (more accurately the Family Poverty Action Group) and later to set up the Low Pay Unit. By the mid-1970s and with the experience gained as a local councillor, he was campaigning for the wholesale transfer of council houses to their tenants.

The purpose of his campaigns was not just to achieve a more equal society by redistributing income and recapitalizing council home tenants but to extend human freedom by removing arbitrary controls and helping people positively to develop their best selves. His interest in poverty in the late 1960s and '70s forced him to read more widely around the issues, something that continued throughout his time as an MP. In constructing this framework of ideas he describes himself as 'self-taught' and 'educated by footnotes', as he invariably followed up references in articles and books, which provided sources for further reading and led on to new areas of study.

Frank's political views and his Christian faith continued to develop alongside each other throughout his life. This relationship between the two was complex, but three influences are clear: first, the works of early Christian socialists such as F. D. Maurice, Charles Kingsley and J. M. Ludlow; second, his discovery of a book of essays written by a group of young Anglo-Catholic clergy teaching at Oxford University, *Lux mundi* (1899), which launched a new era in Anglican thought; and third, a group of British philosophers in the late nineteenth and early twentieth century such as T. H. Green, Bernard Bosanquet and F. H. Bradley, associated with the school of Idealism, and opposed to the Realism of G. E. Moore, Ludwig Wittgenstein and Bertrand Russell in Cambridge.

The philosophy of Idealism, as taught by T. H. Green, a fellow of Balliol College and later professor of moral philosophy at Oxford, had an immense impact on generations of Oxford undergraduates, including H. H. Asquith, Clement Attlee, William Beveridge, Arnold Toynbee and J. B. S. Haldane as well as the founders of Toynbee Hall and the Settlement movement. Idealism opposed the individualism of capitalism and its demoralizing effect on workers. The Idealists were communitarians who saw the state in the form of local and national government as a moral institution which would help individuals make the best of themselves. Morality was not just an individual concern but a social one: to act morally was to take the interests of others into account and to work not for private gain but for the common good. They recognized the role of mediating structures such as the family, village, school, church and charitable institutions, as well as the state, in strengthening the bonds that made up society. Their ideal was the active and responsible citizen, hence their concern to strengthen citizenship.

Many of the Idealists came from religious backgrounds but, like T. H. Green, they rejected Christian dogma while embracing Christian ethics. They did not dispense with religion. They believed that every society had an irreducible spiritual core and so, despite their individual differences, they saw religion as important in providing values that led to the flourishing of communities. Doing good for others was a form of religious observance but without the baggage of Christian doctrine. For Frank this philosophy provided the means to follow the teaching of Jesus 'to love one's neighbour as oneself', but without publicly encumbering it with the command that preceded it, to 'love the Lord God with all your heart, soul and mind'.

Although the founding Idealists were not religious, their ideas had a major impact on the group of young theologians who contributed to *Lux mundi* (1889), edited by Charles Gore, later bishop of Oxford, which set in train a new era of Anglican theology.

The intention of *Lux mundi* was 'to put the Catholic faith in its right relation to modern intellectual and moral problems'. Stated in this way, it was clear that the objective was not to explore how far these ideas might be compatible with accepted Catholic doctrine. That was left to John Henry Newman and others. This practical approach appealed to Frank. The major contributors were not just politically left of centre but socialist in their views, repudiating *laissez-faire* for its individualism and stress on competition, and committed to reducing inequality and injustice through the pursuit of the common good. Charles Gore and Henry Scott Holland, who were both contributors, founded the left-wing Christian Social Union, campaigning against low wages, poor working conditions, slum housing and glaring inequality. In terms of their political values they built on the early Christian Socialists.

Although he was very much influenced by the British
Idealists and the *Lux mundi* group, Frank never referred
to himself as a Christian Socialist and objected to being
categorized as such. The idea that Christianity is the
theory of which socialism is the practice was, he felt,
insulting to Christians of other political persuasions and
parties. He was simply a member of the Labour Party
and committed to its values. Like the Idealists, he was
critical of *laissez-faire* capitalism, but he also recognized
that a market economy created jobs and had the potential
to provide prosperity for all. For him, second- and third-
generation socialists such as R. H. Tawney and William
Temple had too idealistic and optimistic a view of
human nature and of society. They wanted a harmonious
society, modelled on a medieval concept of the just price
and wage, guild socialism and the regulation of trade and
economic life by the Church, a world which they thought
could once more be established in the green and pleasant
land of twentieth-century England. The blueprint
for their views, was a report titled *Christianity and
Industrial Problems*, commissioned by the archbishops of
Canterbury and York in 1916 and substantially written
by Tawney.

Frank believed that the report neglected the serfdom and
economic stagnation that existed in medieval social and
economic structures and which had held people back for
centuries. Similarly, while he accepted the thrust of William
Temple's *Christianity and the Social Order*, published in

1942, which became the basis for the Attlee government's economic and social policies, Frank remained critical of Temple's utopian reforms outlined in the Appendix to that book.

Underlying this was Frank's view of human nature as fallen but capable of redemption. This was the thread running through all his political ideas and all his campaigns, something he termed 'self-interested altruism'. Altruism by itself was not a sufficient basis for political programmes. To succeed, they needed to go with the grain of human nature. It was this which led him to advocate an insurance-based rather than a means-tested, tax-based welfare system and was similar to the form originally advocated by William Beveridge for the welfare state set up by the Attlee government.

Frank won the Birkenhead seat in the 1979 general election, and held it in 1983, but only after he had faced the 'dark days' of reselection to be the Labour candidate at the general election. After this painful experience Frank began to study in much greater depth the life and teaching of Jesus in the Gospels. More than once he said ,'I came late, very late to the Bible.' It was a key step on his journey from the darkness of the problems that confronted him to the light of the God who he believed was at the centre of all things. For him the heart of the New Testament was the Incarnation: the coming of the Kingdom of God. The more he read, the more he felt impelled to clarify his ideas and write down in a systematic way the relationship between his Christian faith and his politics, the result of which was the publication of *The Politics of Paradise* in 1987.

While Christians from every major tradition of the Church, in addressing political and social issues, start with theological principles and then apply them to the issue in question, Frank moved the other way. He always started with the problem. It is an approach described by Dietrich Bonhoeffer in a letter to his friend Eberhard Bethge, the day after the failure of the 'July plot' to assassinate Hitler. He talked about 'the profound this-worldliness of Christianity'. He went on: 'by this-worldliness I mean unreservedly living in life's duties, problems, successes, failures, experiences and perplexities. In so doing we throw ourselves completely into the arms of God, taking seriously not our own sufferings but those of God in the world, watching with Christ in Gethsemane' (Bonhoeffer to Bethge, quoted in Marilynne Robinson, *The Death of Adam* (1998)). Frank was an example of a 'this-worldly' Christian, and it is his 'this-worldliness' which inspired his spiritual journey to explore Christian philosophy and finally to the eyewitness accounts of the Gospels themselves.

Frank's campaigns for reform were an example of 'the profound this-worldliness' of his Christian faith. All his campaigns follow a similar pattern. They invariably start with a problem, generally a person or people who need help: a family unable to provide for itself, a complaint of lack of repairs while canvassing in a block of council flats, a boy aged two, obviously hungry, with his embarrassed grandfather at a food bank, victims of modern-day slavery relating the hell they had been through. Having identified a need, Frank then followed the example of the early Christian Socialists and devoted himself to corralling others with expertise in the subject to undertake meticulous empirical research. This required seeking out three or four influential individuals as trustees who would help to provide money. It was important that there was an advisory body of 'the great and the good': Viscount Runciman for child poverty, Baroness Butler-Sloss for modern-day slavery, Dame Frances Cairncross for schools.

Frank was an excellent communicator, using the media readily to draw proper attention to a campaign. He was never satisfied with short-term remedies for the problems he encountered but set out through legislation to put new structures in place that would have long-term beneficial effects. He had neither the temperament nor the sympathy with the way government works to be a successful minister, and only lasted just over a year as Minister for Welfare Reform (May 1997–July 1998). In all his campaigns he was in reality the executive chair. He was in charge, and he chose the team who would work with him. In government such choices are limited. He was, however, a parliamentarian through and through. He loved the House of Commons and used his position as a backbench MP to effect permanent change. He leaves behind a record of achievement that would be the envy of many who have served on the front benches.

Frank is an outstanding example of Christian service in public life, concerned to fight poverty and injustice in pursuit of the common good. His life has demonstrated what one dedicated individual can achieve to change the lives of the disadvantaged. This book is a celebration of his life and work. Not all will agree with every reform for which he fought, but Frank's compassion and sense of justice are both an example and an inspiration to each one of us. Nevertheless, the very fact that he felt the need to write this book to explain himself to the world raises some tough questions.

Frank was under no illusion but that his progress as a politician was hampered by his being known later in his career as a Christian. Can one declare oneself as a Christian today in elective politics? Frank's soul searching on his political journey will strike a chord with many Christians involved in public life. Initially his faith and politics were related, but rather distantly. The more he read, the more he recognized that Christian faith is more than just a private matter. It is a worldview, and as a worldview it stands apart from other worldviews: secular liberalism, Marxism, libertarianism, pantheism. At each stage on the journey there will always be a force compelling the Christian to move closer to the centre, to Christ and His Kingdom.

IDEAS AND IMAGES

Political Manoeuvres Begin

Here I was, a sixth-former, sitting alone on the top of a bus taking me to school. I was wrestling with a wave upon wave of feeling sick that began once I realized I was leaving a political harbour I had known all my life. I was 15, but these 15 years were the only years I knew. I had grown up in a working-class household where, as key political issues entered the debate, it was clear that both my parents voted Tory. It was natural, therefore, that I should share their scepticism for politicians who favoured too much reform while providing little idea of how the New Jerusalem would be safely built, let alone paid for. The political household of my home taught me also, as if by osmosis, that governing was difficult. My parents' general scepticism, and the realization that doing politics successfully was more difficult than many ever imagined, have never left me.

It never occurred to me that, when all the dust had settled, my political destination would be the Liberals, no matter how attractive Jo Grimond was to the sixth-former who eagerly read daily the *News Chronicle*. Would my new harbour be the Labour Party? And what, then, would this other country be like?

One school acquaintance was a member of the Young Socialists in Chiswick, the town where I had spent all my days, apart from some weekends and all the holidays at our bungalow in Ashingdon in Essex.

It is woeful of me that I now cannot remember the name of my schoolmate, but I see him so clearly. Taller than me, much thinner, pure white skin and a wonderful mop of red hair. He was a year below me, but I knew he was much cleverer.

This schoolmate and I felt strongly about the wickedness of apartheid. No doubt many others of our years did too, but they were not visible. A centre-left coalition – the Anti-Apartheid movement – was calling for a national campaign to boycott South African goods.

My schoolfriend gained the leaflets for the two of us to distribute. I think he printed them himself. They were a simple black-and-white effort telling of the evils of apartheid and pleading with people not to buy South African goods. Outside the local Co-op we stood on a few Saturday mornings handing out our leaflets. I didn't like leafleting then, and I am not too fond of such activity now. The Chiswick Co-op was then opposite what had once been the town's plague pit, and I remember then wondering about whether I was burying my past with the Young Conservatives whom I had joined. We chose the Co-op believing it would be favourable territory for us. I was surprised at the hostility: Labour's vote even then had a distinct 'red wall' aspect.

Sitting on that bus journey, I had no idea that my leaving the YCs would be so ungracious. This was a time before Prime Minister Harold Macmillan said the days of empire were limited in his momentous 'Winds of Change' speech, during a tour of Africa. While Macmillan addressed African leaders, the clever old maestro also aimed his comments at that extreme group of right-wing Tory backbenchers back home. This group of Monday Club members and fellow travellers saw only betrayal in governmental changes in Africa.

The reactions to my leafleting, which represented my first independent political stance, were swift. Over the next few weeks and months I was sent to Coventry by local Young Conservatives who I'd thought of as friends. All the YCs were years and years older than me, or so it seemed then. The men had done national service. They were in their mid-twenties. This was at a time when the YCs were renowned as being the best marriage market in Europe, hence their age profile.

I was now excluded from what was deemed to be any serious conversations. I was hurt by their action. My reaction was quick and lasting. I had no wish to continue to be a YC if this show of intolerance was how they were going to behave in response to what was, in reality, a pathetic little attempt on my part to try and influence the action of local electors in their attitude to the South African regime.

This was a time, however, when deeper loyalties were stirring within me. I was beginning to think about how to

21

translate what I believed into political action, and to judge what I believed against Labour's programme.

My dismissal from the Labour Party 60 years later was even more curt than the one received at the hands of the Young Conservatives. I had resigned the Labour Party whip in Parliament over the active protection of thugs by Jeremy Corbyn's National Executive Committee (NEC), which resulted in bullying behaviour becoming the norm against anyone deemed to be unsound on the issue of Jeremy Corbyn. I also resigned because Mr Corbyn's Labour Party bent over backwards to harbour anti-Semites to such a degree that anti-Semitism had become part of Labour's DNA.

In a two-line statement Mr Corbyn thanked me for 60 years' membership. It was as if I had resigned from the local whist club for showing intermittent commitment during a probationary year's membership. Being a member of the Labour Party was brought to an end by the issuing of that very short comment.

I had left one political party led by Harold Macmillan and was thrown out of one by Jeremy Corbyn. What a contrast. One, Macmillan, was a larger-than-life political actor. The other was smaller than life. One had made politics exciting for me; the other held the prospect of menace.

2

A Sacramental Worldview

I grew up in this parish that I would now call low-church Catholic parish, St Nicholas's in Chiswick. By 'low-church' I mean the liturgy was celebrated in a clear Catholic form, but there was a strong distaste for any excess of church millinery, such as dressing up in yards and yards of lace. Nevertheless, St Nicholas's provided me with a sense of protection and belonging, and I cannot thank this church community enough for the protection it offered me, of which, as I look back, I was so badly in need.

Here I was safe from my father's outbursts of rage and bullying. And here I learned the nature of a wider community that ran alongside the family that my mother provided every day for 'her three boys', as she called us. So, thanks exclusively to her influence, I grew up in a Christian family.

Where St Nicholas's failed me was in the fact that it didn't teach me any idea whatsoever of the Catholic faith, and this lack I became more conscious of as I grew in my sixth form and then moved into university. Strangely, I have always sensed the lacking of a scaffolding of ideas that appeared to be agreed upon by those people I most admire and trust, and whose friendship so enriches my life. I am presented so often as an outsider. If I am so, I am an outsider who longs to be part of the inside. Is this peculiar to me, or is it an integral part of the human spirit as it tries to make sense and order of the events that sweep us along? Whatever the answer, all I know is that during my crucial early years I had no vision of the world into which I could try and fit my life's actions. There was no rulebook to follow. But all too soon I saw this failure as a mighty bonus, a Providential blessing if there ever was one. I was taught to try and think for myself.

Likewise, while there was this marked distaste of church millinery, St Nicholas's lacked much sense of the church militant. This important vacuum was filled much later at university, where the dismissive attitude to Christian Socialism of our outstanding labour history don, John Saville, intrigued me more than any of his Marxist interpretations of nineteenth-century England (and 'England' is not a misprint, despite John's internationalism). The lack of a map or compass from any Catholic rulebook left me deciding for myself what to do on the big and the small issues. I was not too troubled on this score: I did not know then of a different world of structured ideas and philosophies. I still do not fully comprehend this world. Moreover, were not the early followers of Jesus to an important extent in the same position, for where was the method by which he taught? When, as often happened, he was faced with a question, it was often simply to trick him. He replied, 'What do you think?'

Thinking out my position in this universe and trying to make sense of the question 'What is the purpose of life?' began to build the person and the kind of MP I became. I was on my own as far as ideas went. In this most important sense, St Nicholas's served me well. I was taught no catechism or rulebook, let alone a philosophy of life. As a result, I was never in any box from which I had to try and escape and think as though I was on the outside. I was always on the outside.

What St Nicholas's as a church community had failed to teach, its building came to the beginnings of a rescue. This wonderful J. L. Pearson building, which sits proudly at one end of Chiswick Mall, captured two sacramental lessons. First, that the true nature of reality can be greater than our ordinary senses can behold. Pearson is, for me, our greatest Victorian architect. More than any of his contemporaries he was able to defy the expectations one forms about the size and scope of a building's interior based on observations from the outside. Entering through the small choir door, I beheld something for which my eyes had not prepared me. Once inside, St Nicholas's became so much bigger and more significant than it appeared from an external encounter, as is the case, of course, with the Christian story too.

The second sacramental lesson I gained from St Nicholas's was that part of the Christian journey is a movement from darkness into light. By the time I was nine or ten I was trusted to go to church on my own. The safety of children outside their homes then went unquestioned. On some weekday mornings I would be down on the rota to serve at the 7 a.m. or 8 a.m. Mass. If it was a winter's morning, I would be running through the dark to be in church and robed before the said hour.

From the darkness and cold outside I would be welcomed and wrapped immediately by the warmth and the peculiar smell of St Nicholas's. The heating was always turned on during those bleak winter months. But the warmth was more than that artificially created by a pretty efficient heating system: I felt that I belonged there. I was at home. And as I led the priest from the vestry, past the high altar, bowing as we reached the centre, we moved through the darkness into a pool of light that illuminated the Lady Chapel.

While lacking any rulebook to apply to my politics from my grounding at St Nicholas's, I was beginning to learn that a direction of life was an attempt at moving from darkness to light, however feeble that attempt was. The journey would ebb and flow. There would be successes and failures. But there was ever the aim of that goal. I had no detailed rulebook which would hide me from making my own decisions, and particularly the hard decisions about life. This freedom was one of the greatest gifts I could be given for the political and public side of my life.

These two crucial aspects of the Christian faith — of the truth being greater than one's mind can possibly perceive, and that life's journey is an attempt to move from darkness to light — taught me the limits of rationalism, though I was not conscious of it at the time. My introduction, therefore, to these Christian beliefs and, with them, to the limits of rationalism was my first introduction to the politics of Michael Oakeshott and his emphasis on the danger of rationalism in politics. Oakeshott's great inaugural lecture on political education was simply a brilliantly written expansion of the lessons I was already being taught.

With this gift about knowledge that we are on a great journey, both as individuals and collectively, also came a sense of Providence. And here is one of those baffling or conflicting aspects that characterize my life. This sense of Providence, and the feeling of protection that came from it, were given to me very early on. It didn't excuse me from making judgements about what were strategic goals, and what were the best means of achieving these goals. In no sense was I to think that my life was on auto-drive. Activity is the cornerstone of being a Christian and a responsible citizen. This gift of a Providential blessing gave me a sense of being protected, and I've had that feeling as long as I have thought about the purposes of life and of death.

Until recently, I've never been able to see this blessing being on a par with the experience of those Christians who talk of knowing Jesus. I have no such personal knowledge of the Godhead. Looking back now, however, I am not so sure that I did not have the best deal. For most of my life I've envied (I hope not in a corrupt way) those that had the certainty of knowing Jesus. But I shall go into death trusting that the decision I have made about what makes most sense to me will be shown to be true.

3

Human Nature in Politics: Self-Interested Altruism

Here is another baffling aspect of my life. When I went up to university, I was only just into my 18th year, and I was very, very young for a 17-year-old. I had never undertaken any serious work. St Clement Dane Grammar School ensured that as sixth formers we would pass our A-Levels in some sort of fashion.

Like fellow students at St Clement Dane's sixth form, I wished to apply to a number of red-brick universities. Oxford was never mentioned in our sixth form. A lesson here for getting staff, and then students, to raise their expectations of what some students may be capable of achieving.

Students requested an entrance form from each university to which they wished to apply, which needed to be completed and then countersigned by each pupil's form master. I had devoted myself to developing the most fulfilling curriculum of fun while I was in the sixth form, with much of the fun directed at my sixth-form master. I teased him unmercifully. His pomposity was difficult to take. The boot was now, however, firmly on the other foot. After morning registration, those of us who were applying to university, and had forms to be completed that day, made our way to our form master, who sat on a slightly raised dais. When the time came for me to present my forms, they were torn up and thrown back in my face. The form master would scoff 'You, You, YOU, GOING TO UNIVERSITY? How absurd!'

This behaviour made up my mind, if ever it needed making up. Going to university as the first person in your family is a leap into the unknown, something unappreciated by those with parents who are graduates. That unknown horror of leaping into the unknown quickly became less than the humiliation I was subjected to by my sixth-form master's behaviour.

On the day the Hull University forms came, my form master was ill with one of his sniffling colds. Off I went to our economics master, requesting him to complete the form for me. I stood over him as the process was completed and then I went off with my prize to the school Royal Mail letterbox.

Hull gave me an offer. Most students then at Hull thought the university was the pits; it was so often their university of last choice. For me it was my only choice. Once there, I genuinely believed that no other university had such a talented series of politics lecturers, and because Hull was small in student numbers, they knew each of us individually.

I did not begin any serious work until well into my second year at university, when one of the lecturers, Dr Robert Dowse, challenged me, asking why I messed around all the time and didn't use those brains that I had been given. Until that point I never thought anyone would be interested in judging how my intellectual potential might differ from what was traditionally judged as important. I was most interested in seeing the lateral connections between ideas, how one idea could help develop another and, as I learned later, how important this was in developing successful political strategies. From the day when Bob Dowse posed the question of why I did not try to match my work record with the brains he thought I had been given I have always sought to spend my time more effectively than the day before. I fail, of course, but I continually renew that effort.

Not surprisingly, therefore, my 'thinking' when I went up to university about the great themes of why we are here, of life and death, our nature and destiny as men and women, was no better than rubble. But amid that rubble was what would become quite simply the cornerstone of my thinking, namely, my understanding of human nature as it operates in politics, as it does in life generally. Both my parents, as I've said, were working-class Tories. I was never in any doubt then about our fallen nature. However, from my mother came the blessing of being taught not simply about mankind's fallen nature but, equally importantly, of our means and hope of redemption. It was my mother who gave me this rich understanding of our characters.

Here was also the ever so important approach of balancing one great idea against another, if one was to avoid an unbalanced and even an extremist argument. It was taught by the best teaching method ever: by the way my mother lived her own sacrificial life. So here, thankfully, was that cornerstone ready to be hewn into shape. But that cornerstone was carved in a particular way, emphasizing that our fallen natures had to be seen alongside the possibilities of our redemption. This taught me the key lesson about how best to seek truth and also how to practise democracy. Heresy comes so often not by spreading falsehoods but by the assertion of a single truth, and running that truth in isolation from any balancing second truth. This is equally true of politics when arguments have so often to be balanced and weighed. It is the crucial part of the DNA of successful, non-fanatical political action. It applies, of course, to all human activity, but that is not the subject matter here.

The right is forever overemphasizing our fallen nature, to the exclusion of any idea about our redemption. Likewise, the left is overwhelmingly prone to stress that aspect of our character that has been redeemed – not even in a state needing redemption – and does so all too often at the exclusion of the fallen side of our nature. Politics for me has to start from our fallen nature, and not from the state that will be achieved once we are redeemed. Political reforms for me are about making pathways to that perfection. Not to counterbalance the base side of our natures with the possibility and the reality of redemption can for democrats only lead to the politics of cynicism, despair and, of course, failure.

It is from the belief about our character, fallen and yet with the Christian hope of redemption, that I developed the most important of all the working political principles that determined my politics: the idea of self-interested altruism. And given the importance I have attached to countering poverty, here was, in particular, the alpha and omega for my politics of welfare reform. The genesis of my idea about self-interested altruism took clearer shape during the early period working at the Child Poverty Action Group (CPAG), from 1969 onwards. Self-interested altruism became the linchpin that held together in a working relationship the dual nature of our characters. From a very early age I could see this principle of human conduct operating, but given that I had no one who would be interested in my thoughts on the principles of reform that needed to last for the longer term, I kept my thoughts to myself. It was only later, when I began working for CPAG at the age of 27, that I had reason to begin publicly to flesh out this idea.

Two great forces, each opposed to the other, helped shape me as I strove to build my own primary principles of welfare reform. One force came from the left, bearing the name of Professor Richard Titmuss. Mrs Thatcher personified the other, from the right. I was at odds with the wisdom preached by both individuals.

My early years as an MP overlapped with the Thatcher years. The centre-left did continually cry that she 'cultivated greed'. That cry had more than a ring of truth to it, but her ideas were more subtle than this assertion allowed. As I tried to make sense of the Thatcher years, I began to see more clearly the difference between self-interest, selfishness and greed. In particular, self-interest and selfishness were not the same motive force, and selfishness was different from greed. They could at some stage merge one into another. Where Mrs T failed was where all too many reformers in government fail – they try to rush at things and, in her case, she failed to see the need to guard the barrier between self-interest on one side and selfishness and greed on the other.

The crucial distinction between these three aspects of our character became blurred in the public mind. Mrs T, in her determination to reform Britain, which she saw as teetering on the brink of chaos, pulled the pendulum too far in her direction. Yet self-interest on its own was, and is, a pure motive. Indeed, the human race would not survive without it. We are told in the New Testament to love others as ourselves, not less and certainly not more. It was this aspect of our character that got lost as Mrs T's mission developed.

The centre-left's response to what they saw as the cultivation of greed was to give greater importance to the idea that the finest moral position was to 'put the needs of others before our own'. This never washed with me.

But whatever criticism one makes about Labour's totally unrealistic view of human nature in politics, it did stand for a generous human spirit, and without this spirit even the objectives of the best reforms are easily lost. So self-interest had to play the most fundamental part in shaping any successful long-term political reform. Without it, the political house was built on sand.

Here the second great force shaping my perspective was the politics of Richard Titmuss, by far and away the most important developer of the discipline of Social Policy in this country. Richard's ideas had captivated the Labour Party, which with the demise of the adherence to, let alone the practice of, Christianity had been in search of a new morality. As I began my work with CPAG, and because my ideas began to be expressed in opposition to the kind of socialist society Titmuss presented, I will take a little time to develop and contrast our positions, as is so commonly done with essay questions.

The capitalist system produces the wealth that makes and underpins the standard of living in this country. It is not the only force, of course, but it is the most powerful. Social policy aims to make good the inequalities and wickedness that capitalism sometimes drags in its wake: awarding money and services to those that are put at risk, disadvantaged or ground down to breaking point by the working of the capitalist system. Yet it is the same capitalist system that produces the wealth to finance this redistribution and ambulance-type help to those that who lose out most by how the economy works. Thus the different kinds of redistribution go under the title of 'social policy'.

The central belief underpinning the Titmuss School was that a welfare state could run with altruism as its driving force. The most virtuous of human beings, I accept, could, and do, operate on this principle. Still, I believe with all my very being that this is a most unsafe assumption upon which to try and operate politics in general, and a welfare state in particular.

This conviction of pure altruism as the basis of welfare is most clearly epitomized in Titmuss's book *The Gift Relationship*, which also illustrates his brilliance in taking a single example to shine a critical light on how capitalism works in practice.

In this book Titmuss contrasts the NHS Blood and Transplant Department – a gift by one citizen to another in which neither party can possibly know the identity of the other – with the American market in blood. The British service is based, he says, on altruism: citizens gave an unknown and unknowable citizen the lifegiving gift of blood. It was not only morally superior – a gift – but was also safer, as no one with infected blood, but very short of money, was under any incentive to participate, as has been the case in the US.

Long after Richard's book was published, the safety of the blood given to the British transfusion service was made all too clear. Imported blood products from the US had been made from infected blood. The outcome was total devastation for those fellow citizens who contracted HIV from contaminated blood products, and their families were then left to grieve in an atmosphere which saw their neighbours condemning them as social outcasts. My response to this horror was to call for an inquiry and compensation for victims of this infected blood – a campaign that was quickly taken up by the *Sunday Times*.

Inspired by the altruism on which the British Blood and Transplant Department is built, Titmuss allowed the values of this very particular part of the welfare state to be promoted as the core value of the whole welfare state. There can be no doubt to me which is morally superior: altruism, of course, rather than the market. But the example of the British blood transfusion service misled, rather than informed, a robust debate about how human nature in its fallen state is the dominant, although not the only, player in political activity. Altruism alone cannot be the basis all of the time.

Here, as a Christian, I try to make the distinction between love and justice. If we are fortunate, we live in a close association with a few people where actions are determined solely by love (although not all of the time, or as much as we would like them to be). Once we come away from our family and a smallish number of our closest friends, where love can find it easiest to operate and move into the wider world, practically all of us have to operate in terms of justice, if we wish to act fairly and in a principled manner.

The central belief underpinning much of the Titmuss school was that a welfare state could run on altruism. Giving welfare as a gift of love or altruism sounds an extraordinarily wonderful venture to that liberal and usually well-heeled part of the electorate whose role adds a much-needed idealism to our politics. But given our human nature, such a welfare state will be exploited, particularly since the extraordinary common culture forged at wartime, which bound so many of us together on a great common venture, began to break down in the early post-war years, and perhaps even earlier. Those who are strategically placed to see the worst side of each of us – our neighbours – know exactly the limits that have to be enforced to prevent that nation from being taken for a ride.

Titmuss had not only pitted human nature against his kind of welfare state, an error of judgement, but he undermined that judgement still further through the economic assumptions on which his welfare state was being built. Here Titmuss's assumption was plainly daft.

Titmuss believed that we were on the edge of abundance, so it was pointless to worry about, let alone enforce, the work ethic and, to a lesser extent, to counter fraud. The aim was not therefore to limit welfare, as we have done historically, but to find ways of giving it away on an ever-increasing scale. Some assumptions, you might think, after a decade or so of austerity, and particularly so for those dependent for their income on the welfare state.

The worked-out principle of self-interested altruism has been fundamental to my politics generally and to my views on welfare reform in particular. Here altruism is held in balance with self-interest: that is, will reform of the status quo benefit me also, if not immediately, then at some stage of my life? If reforms are to have any chance of success over the very long term, individuals' payments now need to be matched by the belief that benefits to which people are required to contribute will be open to them in the fullness of time. On this basis, and this basis alone, individuals may be prepared over the longer term to support and pay for reforms, and to pay for them when they don't immediately benefit.

This view on self-interested altruism has always pushed me towards a welfare system based on national insurance. Under such a system you gain benefits only after you have made adequate contributions. Likewise, you pay in while others will be drawing out, knowing that at some stage of your life you will be drawing benefits. Tory and Labour governments have moved in the opposite direction to a contributory welfare state. Both parties in government have regularly increased the scope and dominance of means-tested welfare.

I further believe that the more successful one is in extending and strengthening a national insurance welfare state, the easier it is to ask the electorate for acts of altruism for those who fail the insurance test. But this act of pure altruism has to be limited at any one time to a minority of the non-payers. In contrast, once we have a welfare state where the link between past contributions and present eligibility for benefits is broken for the majority of claimants, that welfare state is easily under attack from the right, who always push for welfare cuts. And so the Thatcher era showed.

4

Christian Socialism: God is Everywhere or Nowhere

Christian Socialism was a significant force that swept over the seabed of my ideas, giving them greater shape and character. Although I am often referred to as a Christian Socialist, I do not identify myself thus. I reject the proposition that any political organization can lay claim to a monopoly on Christianity, as do some on the Christian right and left. Moreover, my reading of Christian Socialism is somewhat different from that of many of those groups who campaign under this slogan. Yet these ideas are an important part of the mix that go to making up the map and compass I have acquired for this life's journey. For me, both the ideas and, in particular, the way the second generation of Christian Socialists organized themselves as a pressure group campaigning against poverty have been of great significance. I also rejoice in being able to 'know' a group of Idealist Christians whose lives spilt over into the century during which I was born.

As I have said, the most distinguished and principled Marxist I met at university was John Saville, who taught me and many generations of labour history students. Delivering his lectures and seminars in a somewhat haughty, upper middle-class voice, Saville was dismissive of Christian Socialists' thinking. He never once considered that they were a group that was, like him, trying to make sense of the new industrial world and how best to fight the evils of capitalism's excesses, albeit with a different ideology from him, by drawing on Christian truths. Granted, of course, John was also more interested in replacing capitalism than assuaging its gross injustices. Saville's dismissal of this political tradition left me intrigued about this group, who believed they were doing Christian politics.

It did not immediately intrigue me enough, however. It was well after my university days that I began to read and be thrilled by the Christian Socialist texts, although many of them were far from an easy read. At the start of the Christian Socialist movement in this country are for me three great pioneers, each of whom brought different skills to the movement: F. D. Maurice, Charles Kingsley and J. M. Ludlow.

F. D. Maurice I found too difficult to read at length in the original. Thomas Carlyle remarked that reading Maurice was like trying to eat pea soup with a fork. However, Maurice appealed to me in part as the most important person in the nineteenth century to reignite a particular debate about the afterlife. He argued powerfully against the doctrine of eternal damnation and a belief in hell fires as a means of social control. Maurice proclaimed that we are not just born to be condemned: we were here also to be redeemed. He got very little thanks for his efforts: King's College London, where he held a professorship, sacked him. It was Maurice who made those phrases about eternal hellfire seem so preposterous that most of us today are freed from their dominion. True, there would be a judgement of our record, but the bleakness of a Christianity that divided us into a few sheep predestined for eternal blessings and a multitude of goats headed for damnation no longer held the sway it had before he began speaking out. We are all free to determine our destiny.

Maurice was appealing in a second sense as he was a forerunner for one of those aspects of English Idealism that has proved so attractive to me. While Maurice thought theologically, I thought politically. Each great movement of thought, Maurice argued, bore some witness to the truth. Perhaps that is going a little too far in respect of every set of ideas. My political approach has been to be open to ideas in other parts of the political debate where I think there is justice in their case; Maurice tried to incorporate what he saw as different parts of the truth being proclaimed from various parties within the Church and those who were not part of established Christianity in his own times. Maurice had proclaimed that Jesus had established the Kingdom of Heaven on earth. This was of major importance to the development of my own political philosophy.

At the centre of Maurice's political ideas was the belief that we are created for forms of co-operation rather than *laissez-faire* competition. This has been a belief shared by all ethical socialists.

Maurice's two earliest followers were Charles Kingsley and J. M. Ludlow. Kingsley became a supreme publicist for those earliest of Christian Socialist ideas and practices about improving life chances for the downtrodden – the vast majority of the population at that time. Ludlow brought the money to finance the alternative to capitalism: a new world of co-operatives. A series of co-ops were established, and each of them failed, at least in part because the reformers believed in a much more noble view of human nature than perhaps history presents. Here was the basis of a successful political model – the ideas (Maurice), a supreme publicist (Kingsley) and the money to put some of these ideas into practice (Ludlow). I have tried to follow this co-operative model by drawing on an array of different talents for each of the campaigns in which I have been involved. I have also sought, particularly in the early campaigns, to borrow status when needed as a force to marshal power behind long-term, sustainable reforms.

Most records and textbooks on politics ignore the role of borrowed status as a force in politics and certainly in pressure group politics, where it can be most effectively employed. Regrettably, politics in Britain remains very much an elitist activity, although, as Brexit showed, far less than it once was. Elites still count. Elites speak to elites. Those who do not have this status need to borrow it from those who do when trying to get other elites to concede reform.

For me, borrowing or borrowed status has been fundamental. How could I continue to campaign on themes with which voters had become somewhat bored and spark a new interest? Renewed interest could come, of course, from new facts. But that interest could also come from new personalities – those whom the public wouldn't immediately expect to see associated with a poverty campaign. This ranged from bishops, in those very early days, to trade unionists (acting together as a political force on the TUC's economic council, as it then was), right through to Harry and Meghan opening a citizens' supermarket in Birkenhead and declaring, by their presence, their interest in abolishing hunger and destitution as we know it today for poorer people in Birkenhead and in the wider world as well.

If my interest in Christian Socialism began with a flirtation with Maurice and his associates, it became an affair of the heart once I read, and read about, the volume of essays entitled *Lux Mundi: A Series of Studies in the Religion of the Incarnation*, published in 1889. Here was a group holding on to truth but trying to direct it into new paths which had already been cut by other thinkers. The *Lux Mundi* group, as they were called, grappled with the advances in biblical studies that were being pioneered in Germany, and here in Britain to a lesser extent, and with Darwin's theory of evolution. Both developments seemingly undermined many of the stories in the Old Testament and placed doubt at the centre of Christian experience for so many people. Yet it is where I am. In the wake of these shockwaves, the *Lux Mundi* group of Christian Socialists aimed to present a coherent case for, and rational defence of, Christianity.

The *Lux Mundi* group did more than break with theological convention with their aim to put the Catholic faith, in its right relation to modern intellectual and moral problems, rather than to put such problems in a right relationship to the Catholic faith, as theologians had done since time immemorial. *Lux Mundi* reset the compass for the Christian journey. Instead of the Catholic faith being the lens through which the things of this world were mediated, the world was to be the basis for understanding fully the truths of the Catholic faith.

Here, dear reader, I hope you see why this was an approach that so attracted me. I recalled earlier that at St Nicholas's I was never given much teaching about the Christian faith. Hence my approach had always been to start with an understanding of the world's injustices and then to see what the Christian faith had to give in terms of guidance, motivation and aspiration for action.

This group's revolutionary stance is perhaps best caught for me by their emphasis on the Incarnation of Christ at the expense, somewhat, of His death and resurrection. Under the onslaught of their debate, the balance shifted too far, as it so often does with fundamentally critical but tough reformers. English Church thinkers in the earlier part of the twentieth century overemphasized the Incarnation. Only as the Nazi threat became a living threat to our very existence did the debate gain a better balance between birth on the one hand, and resurrection on the other. The messages of both Christmas and Easter are of equal importance. Christmas teaches us something of fundamental importance about God becoming man, and therefore the importance of this world, while Easter teaches us an equally great truth about the fall of humanity and the means of redemption. Western European theology stressed from the end of the nineteenth century, and way into the early decades of the twentieth century, too much of the Incarnation at the expense of the cross. Christians were therefore largely unprepared to be in total opposition to the Nazi forces as they gathered strength in Germany during the latter part of the 1930s.

The *Lux Mundi* group held importance for me because of their insistence on God's presence in the world, on the immanence of God in every aspect of our daily life. I could no longer hold a view of God being somewhere up there. God had come down to earth and was everywhere or nowhere. If God was everywhere, politics was a crucial activity in our response to this wonderful fact.

The *Lux Mundi* group held a further and equal attraction for me: they established, along with the abolition of slavery, what I regard as among the most effective example of pressure group politics of the nineteenth century.

Following *Lux Mundi*, and its preaching of an incarnational theology, Christian Social Union branches were established in towns around the country to carry out activities that drew attention to the plight and the exploitation of the poor. 'White lists' were drawn up, for example, to tell people of goodwill that, if they bought in a particular shop, they would be purchasing goods not produced by 'slave labour'. The boycotting of shops using slave labour was, as you can imagine, not very popular, particularly by the majority of shop owners who in order to survive undercut the price in other shops and sold goods made by sweated labour. How this campaign has formed the basis for part of today's politics is a question I pick up later, in Chapter 8, in the context of modern slavery.

5

The Kingdom of God

It is rather shocking that I learned about God's immanence through the work of the *Lux Mundi* group and
not through the Bible, but that is a price paid for educating
oneself rather than being educated by the Church. I came
to the Bible relatively late in life, as a further inspiration for
my political career.

Nevertheless, it is the Bible which has become one
of the more important influences on my politics, giving
greater coherence to my work. And yet I rarely mention
it. Why? The answer is quite simply for political reasons:
I wish the campaigns on which I work to be successful.
The Christian language today has sadly become a
barrier to, rather than a purveyor of, meaning. Many
readers may have already given up on the account I am
narrating here, for this very reason. For political success,
it is not a bad start to begin speaking in the tongue that
people understand. But it is from the Bible that I take the
revolutionary basis of my politics: teachings about the
Kingdom of God.

The nature of this Kingdom develops throughout the
Old Testament, responding to the politics of the day. When

the Jews were subjected to the rule of foreign powers,
the Kingdom of God was very much viewed in terms
of personal piety or, as I would call it, virtuous living.
The idea of the perfect society was kept alive by the way
individuals lived their own lives. At other times, when the
Jews were free of foreign domination, the Kingdom was to
be built and established as an ideal society in this world by
collective political action. The virtuous life and collective
action to establish the Kingdom here in this world are two
approaches to politics. Sometimes it is only possible to
practise the virtuous life. At others, circumstances permit
both to be pursued simultaneously. The virtuous life has a
collective function too.

Whatever interpretation the Kingdom had in Jewish
teaching, the view through time was always of a Kingdom
of this world. Towards the end of the Old Testament the
message gains momentum and sounds a note of urgency.
The Kingdom is to be established in this world but will be
established from outside the world. We are now firmly in
the New Testament with the historical Jesus, who, through
His presence and His teaching, gives us a threefold
development of this Kingdom. There is first a heralding
of a Kingdom at hand. Then there is His teaching that his
ministry signifies that God has now actively entered into
history in a totally new way. His ministry teaches of a
Kingdom present, and as it is sought, it is enlarged. Finally,
we have the view that this Kingdom is to be completed at
the end or fullness of time.

My revolutionary politics centres on the second and third interpretations of the Kingdom. Jesus' birth heralded a new age for His very life and His presence in the world is the beginning of the Kingdom. By seeking it now through our personal and collective action, we help to expand that Kingdom and we have the promise of its completion at the end of time. While my politics has invariably been part of a collective effort, I wish in no way to downgrade the equal importance of living a virtuous life. Indeed, without such striving I believe no Kingdom worthy of that name can be established.

For I know that socialist institutions cannot operate very differently from capitalist institutions unless one has established the virtuous life on a very wide scale. My great political hero, Clement Attlee, at the close of establishing what he hoped would be the institutional structure of the New Jerusalem, set his colleagues the task of making socialists run the socialist institutions they had finally established. Without the kindly face to greet, and a generous heart to interpret the rules, Attlee thought a socialist state could act as harshly and severely as the capitalist society he was trying to replace. The resolution had to go beyond establishing institutions. It had to be lived if the greatest of the reforms were to be delivered fully.

It is because of this collective political effort that I've never shared Enoch Powell's view that all political lives end in failure, unless we politicians are struck down early or resign at the peak of our stewardship. Enoch's view was characteristically an individualist approach to politics. A collective approach to politics for Christians is one where their collective work is not of defeat at the hands of the individual's death but is a form of politics that promises a final victory.

This sense of a Kingdom being revealed has become my personal and political lodestar and is an approach to doing politics based largely on doubt about the great Christian story. It is, however, a story that makes more sense to me in understanding the world, and our places in it, than any other set of beliefs I've been offered.

6

Freedom, Without Which
All is Lost

Now to the last value that has had a bearing on my
life at almost every turn: freedom. While I have
expressed freedom at work in society through a contract
basis — laying down our duties to society, and in return
receiving a set of rights — I am aware that freedom in the
democratic form we see it today goes back to the cove-
nantal basis of freedom that was established between God
and the people of Israel at Mount Sinai and described in the
book of Exodus. But my own view of what freedom is has
been shaped by the particular circumstances of my home
life in my early years and at university.

I was very conscious from my earliest days that my father
loathed me and that this was the basis of his bullying. I
also did not know when I would be subjected to the next
onslaught. This experience was to turn me from a difficult
child into a child that did not do what I was commanded. It
gave me a most rigorous and important political training. I
stress again that I proved to be a particularly difficult child in
his eyes. His behaviour taught me much about the tyranny

of arbitrary power, as well as about the use of power and how power could be lost. I was 15 when this happened. He came at me with a hammer, which was a unique event. I took the hammer out of his hand and said that if he tried that again, I would use the hammer on him. The balance of power had changed. Before I acted I had no idea that I would prove to be the stronger, but I was. No more physical bullying. Thank God! I never drew properly the lesson from this incident. It is one thing to destroy a power base, but is one prepared to replace it with a better one, and to do so as a 15-year-old?

It also proved to stand me in good stead to oppose the bullying of the Trotskyist tendencies that took over the Merseyside Labour Party, particularly the Birkenhead Labour Party, in the early 1980s. And the bullying of Momentum that followed the same trajectory decades later.

Freedom from the exercise of arbitrary power has been both the simplest and the strongest of all my drives. My support for the sale of council houses, which I discuss in the following section, is based partly on this hatred of the way arbitrary power can crush the best chance individuals and families have to claim some of the fruits of the good life.

Freedom from arbitrary power is, I hope, equally matched by that English Idealist objective of trying to organize politically so that every individual would have the opportunity to achieve their best self. As soon as we reached the English Idealism part of the political ideas course at university, I knew these were 'my' ideas in a way

I had never felt about any other of the grand schools of English political thought.

When English Idealism made its appearance on the British scene through the work of T. H. Green, an Oxford don, and his close associates, it presented Christianity in a form that allowed many Christians to defend their beliefs rationally. Unlike almost all other philosophers, Green and his followers were not seeking to establish a school of philosophers that would take forward their ideas. Instead, the English Idealists' revolution was to be concerned with developing a public ideology to train the next and future generations of the establishment. Idealist politicians centre on how politics should ensure that individual citizens are able to develop their best selves. The impact was considerable, as R. G. Collingwood recalls in his autobiography. Through its teaching 'on the minds of his pupils, the philosophy of Green's school might be found ... penetrating and fertilising every part of the national life'.*

English Idealism also held an attraction for a much wider group of people of goodwill who worried that, with a collapsing Christianity, there would be no agreed ethical ideology to underpin a voluntary policing of society. For this group, English Idealism came to the rescue. It took much of the ethical honey from the Christian hive and

*R. G. Collingwood, *An Autobiography* (London: Penguin Books, 1944), p. 17.

moved it to the safety of hives that were more accessible to the secular world. Idealism therefore appealed to both Christians, for whom the ethic of Christianity was the heart of their belief, and the growing number of non-believers, who grieved at the loss of subscribing to a public ideology based on Christian ethics.

At the centre of the work of English Idealists was the attempt to extend the idea of freedom beyond the negative sense that John Stuart Mill's father had thought, as the freedom from restriction to do things, into the idea of freedom that now most of us understand in this country. Here was the freedom to do things, and the resources to do them, so that each of us should be able to develop their best self. For me, however, the first and most important aspect was to establish a freedom from fear and arbitrary power.

In a discussion with the then Chief Rabbi, Jonathan Sacks, I was gently chided over my political framework for establishing a contract society as I had proposed in a number of my books. Jonathan pointed to the idea of a covenanted society based on the model given in the Old Testament between God and His people of Israel. The keeping of the covenant guaranteed freedom as a central political value of that society. Freedom as a political value as we know it today pre-dates the offerings made by Greek society and is to be found in the earlier parts of the Old Testament.

But can a practising politician offer a covenanted political basis for freedom while simultaneously offering a programme that could win a parliamentary majority in this country? Support has to be built up in steps or stages. Here the two models of political activity offered to us in the New Testament are of such relevance.

There is for sure the light on the hill – in this instance, beckoning us to the ideal of a covenanted society: 'Ye are the light of the world. A city that is set on the hill cannot be hid.' The other political model of the New Testament is where the agent of change becomes lost in the act of helping to secure change. The New Testament gives the example of yeast, which loses its identity in playing an indispensable role in creating the bread we eat. 'The kingdom of heaven is like unto leaven, which a woman took, and hid in three measures of meal, till the whole was leavened.'

For most of my life, I have adopted that New Testament model of politics that requires the action of getting involved with others to bring about change. The need for immediate action is so great, and the policies that need to be adopted are likewise already well thought out. But the light on the hill holds importance too, and for two reasons. First, how can one judge the rightness of an immediate campaign unless one can judge whether the campaign might move society nearer to the ideals signalled to us by the light on the hill? Sometimes, and here is the second importance of the light on the hill as a political activity sketched out in the New Testament, the political agenda is so restrained that the options for favourable short-term reforms are absent. Then, and for me only then, the only option is to adopt the light on the hill political approach. But even in this case one has a duty simultaneously to try and build opportunities from that vision which again inspires the electorate to demand reform, and to begin to build up for that vision a political momentum of its own.

I accept, however, that there are sometimes inadequacies in just this immediate approach. It is therefore important to see one's short-term political activity set within the context of those long-term objectives. It is for this very reason that I have adopted a contributory basis to welfare rather than a means-tested one. A contributory basis is one where there is a clear contract of contributions and duties set out whereby those contributions earn rights. Of course this is far from the ideal. But it measures important steps to that ideal, for I believe that if one can inculcate a contractual basis in society, the rules of the contract so become affairs of the heart that the heart is open to the covenanted approach.

Indeed, here is perhaps a supreme paradox. John Adams drafted the constitution of Philadelphia. The pilgrim fathers and mothers left England for religious reasons. Christian truths were at the centre of their thinking. Yet, when Adams took up his pen to draft the Philadelphia constitution, he wrote not on a covenanted basis between God and the citizen but, as I would call it, a contractual basis between citizen and other citizens, and thereby with the society in which they lived. Adams remarked that it is a social compact, by which the whole people covenants with each citizen, and each citizen with the whole people, that all shall be governed by certain laws for the common good.

For the next sections I have chosen a number of campaigns with which I have been associated. Each campaign, and indeed every campaign I have tried to promote over the past 50 years, has been about extending freedom, either in the sense of being free from arbitrary power or in the positive sense of having the support to develop our best selves. Freedom has therefore been central to the whole of my political activity.

As time has wound its way, I have been surprised by how what is called the negative definition of freedom – freedom from arbitrary power – has become more important. I assumed five decades ago, with rising prosperity, that the campaigns with which I would be involved centring on social justice would be focused exclusively on the positive aspect of freedom. Not so. The dreadful surprise for me has been how much of my time as a politician has been spent on campaigning against slavery in this country and this country's supply chains, as well as to achieve the simple basic objective of my fellow citizens having enough resources to feed themselves. These are examples of my attempt to implement the English Idealists' stress on the need for positive support so that individuals and families have the resources to develop their best selves. And the idea of developing our best selves I see as a universal impulse implanted in the vast majority of human beings. And in developing our best selves, I see a means of seeking the Kingdom.

IDEAS INTO
ACTION

7

Fighting Poverty: Child Benefit, Council House Sales and the Redistribution of Wealth, and the Minimum Wage

In the House of Commons, MPs must declare financial gains in the Register of Members' Interests that could affect their judgement when speaking, voting or lobbying on any issue. Other interests that similarly shape how we behave and act as politicians do not need to be declared. But let me, dear reader, put before you my first declaration of interest.

I have always accepted as a politician that, since the dazzling advent of Freud into public debate, it is foolish for anyone to declare that they know themselves fully, and what we politicians say and write about our motives may be partial, no matter how we struggle to be completely truthful.

During my 50 years of campaigning, bearing Freud in mind, I have aimed to put first what I perceive as the public good, knowing also that my work satisfies a deep need within my very being. Here is the second interest I need to declare. I undertake my work for the same reason that I breathe. It may be that the meeting of one's inner drive, or drives, has been the decisive determinant of my actions. Each of us has these basic drives, and I have tried to direct my basic drive to improve the rough deal so many people in Birkenhead and this country receive. So, to a second declaration.

Each of us, I believe, has a pool of intimate love within us. Much of that pool is given unconditionally and largely unthinkingly to one's immediate family. I have no wife and children, and I have therefore been conscious that this need to love has been spread over a wider area. That love which would have been given to a family I have tried to use to sustain a love for constituency and country. Love of these two objectives, of course, is common to all MPs, I hope, but I had been freer than most MPs to direct my love. I have never had the pressure of ensuring there is money for school uniforms, shoes to be replaced and ever greater food bills as children feed their growing bodies. And I therefore had no fear about ceasing to be an MP because of any disastrous impact on my family. Mortgage payments were never a concern in how I voted. I had never known the natural pressure from wives or husbands who resent the amount of time their partner gives to constituents and to serving our country.

Back, then, to the principles that have shaped my politics and political career and, I hope, more so, to what has been achieved in national and local politics. I began to decide on the case studies of ideas into action that I hope best illustrate my politics and the politician I am. These offer two crucial insights into the influences that have shaped me as a political animal.

The first is that my campaigns on national reforms have invariably been built on individual requests for help. The campaign against Modern Slavery is an example which didn't spring from an individual grievance being brought to my attention. But many constituents' injustices stemmed from a careless and wrong application of a policy that is essentially fair. These injustices can usually be put right without too much effort. Other constituents' pleas for help could not be met within the right application of existing law and practices. In trying to win redress for these individuals' grievances there was also the aim to gain reform that benefited all people who were similarly aggrieved, either through action in Parliament or through the courts. During my time at Child Poverty Action Group (CPAG) that activity was deemed to be a strategy of class actions.

Very few of the reforms I worked for have been top down, thinking up an abstract reform to impose it as a political settlement. That is not my style of politics. My approach is not to think theoretically on what reforms a general theory dictates. The reverse is true. I firmly belong to the British, and particularly the English, school of empiricism, who draw on their own experiences to construct what actions will be best in winning social and political change. Such politics concentrate on identifying the greatest evils of our time and then busying oneself with others in trying to overcome them.

The second characteristic is that practically all of the reforms I have campaigned for have been initiated outside of the Labour Party structure. They have been collectively driven, of course – i.e., with groups of people – but they have been reforms that, from the outset, I attempted to persuade Labour to adopt.

Here are a selection of those campaigns that illustrate the ideas that have driven me. First, the campaign to establish child benefit, then the efforts to make a case for council house sales, followed by the minimum wage campaign. The campaign to tackle hunger and destitution, one to counter the rising tide of modern slavery in this country and the rest of the world and, finally, the need to protect our environment follow in the next chapter.

Child Benefit

There was much laughter during my interview for CPAG's directorship back in 1969. I was sitting in a chair that was placed where a carpet and underfelt had been completely worn away. I had squashed cockroaches on the stairs as I made my way up to the attic at 1 Macklin Street, in London's Covent Garden, to what was then CPAG's head office. 'What do you know about the academic literature on poverty?' 'Not very much' was me being economical with the truth. 'Do you know what the wage stop is?' The wage stop was the rule to prevent claimants from gaining more on benefits than what they would gain if they were following their normal occupation. 'I can spell the term.' And then at last, 'Why do you think we are interviewing you?' 'Because I have a passion for pursuing reforms that favour the poor.' I got the job, just. And 1 Macklin Street, with its cockroaches and smell of rotting dead mice behind my built-in bookcase, became my home for the next ten years.

Two aspects of my decade with CPAG are important to this story. The first was a lobbying strategy that could use political nous as a substitute for the wealth and power base on which traditional lobbying organizations in the British political system depended. The second was also political: did we have strong enough nerves to try to bring down a government, if necessary, or to create mayhem that would be difficult for a government to survive, to prevent the needs of the poor from being ignored?

My first task, however, was to reposition the group. It had set itself up as an appendage to the Labour Party, and for good reason. The Labour government would soon abolish poverty. But this appendage status to the Labour Party was important: the group acted both as the thinking and conscience-making body in respect to social policy in the Labour Party. The history of the 1964–70 Wilson government, however, showed that a Labour government left to its own devices might not deliver an anti-poverty strategy, no matter what yards and yards of rhetoric argued to the contrary about the party's programmes and achievements. Having a one-party lobby group seemed to me to be folly if the party to which one was an appendage could indeed ignore when it wished what CPAG believed to be imperative to an effective anti-poverty strategy. Or if, who knows, that party was unlikely to win power.

To reposition the group from its adolescence into a fully grown-up member of the lobby nexus in British politics was my first task. That repositioning came about through the group's manifesto, *The Poor Get Poorer under Labour.* I had come to my work treasuring the observation of Dick Crossman, in his previous incarnation as a political don. Now, ironically, he was the Secretary of State for Health and Social Services under Wilson, but he had also been a commentator of much note on British politics. Crossman, who was the minister CPAG dealt with, saw the role the party myth played in party politics: it was morale-building and crucial at election time in mobilizing the party faithful to beat the wicked other side. But Crossman's myth gave me a deadly weapon.

I spent my first months at CPAG reading through everything I could on evaluating Labour's programme for the poor. I had come to my task believing that a Labour government would act to abolish poverty. As my notebooks began to show, the Labour government was not doing that well. Hence what became *The Poor Get Poorer under Labour* campaign.

I had a wish to enter Parliament as a Labour MP. The whole of the executive, I guessed, voted Labour and here was the first campaign under my stewardship. I believed, wrongly, that Labour would not go into the next election after we published our memorandum – *The Poor Get Poorer under Labour* – without making major concessions to the poor by increasing family allowances. The family allowance was a benefit established by the wartime coalition government to help mothers and children. CPAG proposed an increase in family allowances and, in order to limit the costs, to decrease, by the same value as the family allowance increase, the value of what were called child tax allowances. These tax allowances were then, generally speaking, drawn by men and not women.

In the run-up to the 1970 election, the Tories promised CPAG an increase in family allowances, but once in office, they failed to deliver. We had a good war against the Ted Heath government in 1970, and the Conservative government could not rebut our charges by simply denouncing our campaign as part of a Labour Party front. Now the group had influence plus some political muscle that it would use, if necessary, to concentrate a government's mind on what it might do for the poor. Poverty as a cause had become a political issue, although we had as yet to deliver to the poor themselves.

How to get those extra resources to poorer families? That was a task the group had in the run-up to the next election, which came in 1974 – when, rather like Number 11 buses, we had two in quick succession. Labour committed itself to introducing the group's proposal of a new benefit entitled child benefit. This benefit had come from the idea of adding the monies paid in family allowances with the revenue lost in granting child tax allowances. After a Herculean struggle, CPAG and others convinced the government that the benefit should be paid in total to the mothers, leaving fathers in work worse off as, with the loss of child tax allowances, their tax burden increased.

The Labour government delivered the Child Benefit Bill on 7 August 1975. The one remaining issue on which the Cabinet had to decide was the rate at which the full child benefit would be paid from the promised date of 1 April 1977. On 5 April 1976 Jim Callaghan replaced Harold Wilson as Prime Minister and all went quiet on the child benefit front, although the Cabinet minutes from this period showed intense activity. Malcolm Wicks, who was then a member of CPAG's executive and a temporary civil servant in the Home Office, had read the minutes, made copies and passed them to me. Malcolm was later to be an MP and Labour minister.

I received a number of instalments from Malcolm and did not act until the story from the minutes was complete – a betrayal by the Labour government of its promise to introduce child benefit. I published the minutes in an article titled 'Killing a Commitment' in the now sadly defunct *New Society*.

All hell broke loose, and so it should have done.

During this most wonderful hue and cry, the Official Secrets Act was evoked to find out who was at the source of the leak. With Malcolm's permission I declared that I had written the article but refused to say who had given me the Cabinet minutes. I was thereby able to direct the campaign quite openly through a number of news bulletins on radio and television. Cabinet ministers and others were fighting like ferrets in the sack trying to suggest they were innocent of the leak, but that maybe a colleague wasn't.

Once I declared the authorship, the hue and cry was now over the issue of whether I should be sent to prison. Was I a Russian agent? Perhaps my bank account should be seized and frozen. And so on with these most absurd suggestions. The government was being beaten up from all sides, from the media campaign led by CPAG, from Labour backbenchers who were furious that it had been suggested to the Cabinet that they were against the scheme – they definitely weren't – and from the Tory opposition who knew then how to oppose. The government retreated. It would introduce child benefit after all.

I was still uncertain that the Labour government would keep to its commitment. So I kept a watching brief – I was, after all, paid to do so.

Around Christmas time of 1977, political correspondents wrote of the post-Christmas meeting arranged at Chequers where ministers were to lay down the guidelines for the 1978 budget. Would the government introduce child benefit at a more generous level than the value of the existing family allowance and child tax allowance? CPAG organized a lobby of trade unions, churches, women's organizations and support among Labour backbenchers, and still we failed to shift the Prime Minister and the Chancellor. I saw there was one last chance to achieve our objective of breaking the will of the Prime Minister and of getting him to desert his Chancellor.

In 1977 the government announced a reduction of tax allowances to help pay for the new child benefit. New codings were therefore devised and sent out to employers. But now the Prime Minister and his Chancellor wanted to kill the child benefit commitment. The government's jugular was exposed. It centred on the fact that the government had still to gain Parliament's approval for reducing child tax allowances. Without that authority the tax codes would have to be changed back if there was no adequate payment of child benefit. I wrote to Anthony (or, as he was better known, Tony) Christopher, who ran the Inland Revenue Staff Federation (IRSF), asking what would happen if the opposition supported Labour backbenchers in preventing the government gaining retrospective authority to amend tax allowance codes. Anthony said that if that occurred, his members, being so overworked, would, he believed, strike.

I asked Tony to write to the Chancellor and tell him that the game was up and that his budget would be in chaos if he did not concede the additional monies for child benefit. Much, much later I learned from Tony that he had copied that letter to the Prime Minister. A couple of days before the budget, the Prime Minister deserted the Chancellor and told him to give in to the demands for the increase in revenue to accompany child benefit.

What lessons did I draw from this extraordinary episode, which changed politics in respect to children? First there was a question of bravery. Malcolm Wicks was incredibly brave in making copies of Cabinet minutes and leaking them to me; without his action there would have been no child benefit. There was, second, the question of luck. Malcolm was a civil servant in the Home Office, and while Jim Callaghan reclassified the Cabinet papers as top secret, nobody had taken any notice and they continued their rounds between departments for relevant civil servants to read.

Third, there was friendship. I knew Tony Christopher right back from my efforts on leaving university to gain a trade union job. I applied for a post in the IRSF, where Tony held a position of growing importance. I did not get the job, but the two of us kept in touch as we turned up at meetings. Fourth, there was co-operation. Labour backbenchers understandably did not want to be the agent to bring down a major piece of their Party's budget. But if the Tories were prepared to take the child tax allowance clause on the floor of the House, where whips would find it so much more difficult to control all Labour members, instead of a handpicked number of members on the Finance Bill committee, Tory and some Labour MPs would go into the same lobby.

Introducing child benefit resulted in the largest direct redistribution of income to poorer families since the introduction of the welfare state. It was not until Gordon Brown proposed the abolition of the 10p rate of tax, hitting low-paid and particularly female workers, that a government was forced to retreat, when I organized both Labour and Tory backbenchers against the move.

Council House Sales and the Redistribution of Wealth

Sometimes, to establish a new consensus on the centre-left, there is a need to shock and, hopefully, to push the debate on to a new reform agenda that advantages the poor. The attempt to redirect the poverty lobby to making the claim that the poor should have capital, and that the capital should be bound up in their council house homes, is one example of an attempt by me that ended in failure. In 1975 I wrote a pamphlet titled 'Do We Need Council Houses?' and argued for their sale. Two Labour Prime Ministers asked civil servants to investigate the feasibility of a proposal – the selling of council houses – which had the aim of becoming the biggest transfer of assets since the Reformation. This time the redistribution was to poorer people, not to the rich. Civil servants reported that it was impossible to implement. That proved not to be so.

Civil servants believed differently under a different Prime Minister. The idea was implemented by an incoming Tory government as part of a right-wing ticket rather than directed on centre-left principles. Mrs Thatcher sold cheaply, and there was no rebuilding of the stock sold; nor was any of the money used directly to repair stock and to build social housing. This case study illustrates that once ideas are out in the open, the right will act if they think there are votes in the proposals, particularly if the left hesitates and stumbles, as it did here. The left chose to be a party of a slogan over the best interests of the poor. Here was a reform that both worked with the grain of human nature and, given changes in why the attitudes on acceptable levels of bureaucracy, a reform whose time had come.

I had for a long time been thinking about the wealth tied up in council houses and about the bureaucratic use of this wealth to reduce tenants to little better than serfs – and serfs who looked to the Lord of the Manor at the Town Hall to direct all too many of their actions. I remember the exact point at which I realized, as a very young councillor representing a Turnham Green ward on Hounslow Council in London, that the centre would not hold and, moreover, that it should not hold.

I was canvassing in a council block of flats. 'See that door, mate? It has kept me awake night after night for two years. Every time the bleeding wind blows, that door bangs and can bang all night. For years I have been complaining to your council but nothing bleeding happens.' My constituent was referring to the door outside his home which led to the stairs.

'Why don't you mend it yourself?' I hesitantly inquired 'and bill the council for the cost. I will register the bill if you want.' 'Blimey, what do you think I pay the rent for?'

The argument went on for a bit before I retreated. As I wandered down those concrete stairs stained with urine I knew the game had to change. And 'game' in the most honourable use of the term. If this gentleman owned his own home, surely his attitude would be different; he would not believe that it was up to somebody else to do what was obviously needed, even though a failure to act, because he paid the rent, affected his quality of life.

Being a member of Hounslow Council's Housing Committee, I had seen tenants struck off the waiting list because of their 'cheek'. Chiswick residents were sometimes offered accommodation, but not those right at the other end of the borough, in Feltham, despite tenants claiming that this would make it impossible to travel to their current jobs which were to the east of Chiswick. Their response was deemed to be insolent. The Housing Chair, who would always take his teeth out at the beginning of a meeting and lay them out on a beautifully laundered white handkerchief, would bang the table as the tenants were struck off the list for their audacity in refusing a council offer. And his teeth would jump as if in anger at 'these people' getting beyond their station in life.

This treatment of council house tenants was part of the reason why I began marshalling the case for the sale of council houses. As a member of the Housing Committee, and being interested in longer-term trends in revenue and investment, I looked at council housing expenditure as a percentage of national income, and of council rents in particular, and at whether there was scope to improve the quality of housing, while adding to the stock of housing, if these trends continued. The trends were all going in the wrong direction to achieve either one, let alone both, of these objectives. The question therefore became: what rules should be changed to get the proportion of national income for council housing to increase rather than fall? If we were to build more houses and improve the existing stock – for example, by having secure door entries and carpeted stairs, which were so badly needed in the block of flats I was leaving – what had to change?

In 'Do We Need Council Houses?' I outlined a programme to set the serfs free. I used the most emotive terms I could, so as to shock the 400 or so delegates to the Catholic Housing Aid Society's annual conference held in June 1975, and a wider audience beyond.

What would working people give to own their own homes? The data showed that those in the best homes rarely, if ever, moved. Children had the right of succession. The best homes were rarely going to come onto the council's lettings market, so they were never going to be up for grabs for families on the waiting list. But might they, I asked, not be bought at a top price if the whole family clubbed together to acquire a family asset? The family would know they would benefit when the parents died and the assets were transferred to the children and possibly sold. I also proposed a stipulation that all the monies gained thereby should be used to build new and repair existing stock.

'Do We Need Council Houses?' was my first attempt to argue that countering poverty was much more than the poor having more immediate money, crucial as this is. The poor, like the rich, needed assets that would free them from the arbitrary rule of officialdom, as well as providing them with collateral for other transactions which could markedly increase their freedom. I also had another political objective. It was to convince working-class Labour voters that we were on their side and would change the rules in order to satisfy their legitimate aspirations for home ownership, which was then beyond the reach of most of them under the existing rules.

While Labour audiences gave me the worst possible kicking for promoting this heresy, they couldn't have known of Labour's attempt to adopt this idea. As we have seen, not only did Prime Ministers Wilson and Callaghan ask civil servants to see if a Labour government could implement such a scheme. The idea was also supported from the inside by Joe Haines, Prime Minister Wilson's press secretary, who had similar ideas. Even so, the civil servants reported that it was an impossible reform to make good. So there the idea rested, although it was now part of the political agenda. That agenda was being shaped also by Peter Walker, the future Thatcher Cabinet minister, who published the idea around the same time as I did. His scheme had one crucial difference, however. It was to sell off cheap to win over working-class Labour voters. When Mrs Thatcher gained power four years later, she asked for a group of civil servants who could make the idea possible. The rest is history, of course, except that Mrs Thatcher sold cheap and the monies were used to cut taxation. The Tories subsequently gained the votes I hoped Labour would keep and Labour was labelled as being against extending freedom and, worse still, being on the side of bureaucratic control.

What political lessons should be gained from this initiative? I never gained Labour's agreement to what became the biggest transfer of wealth and one that could help the poor most in the beginnings of a totally new strategy to counter poverty. And so it proved with a whole run of reforms that I have promoted on wealth. If wealth is good enough for the rich, then it is certainly good enough for the poor. Wealth, in Bacon's words, is like muck: to do its job well, it needs to be spread. I failed with proposals to spread that muck or wealth, or whichever term you prefer. My proposal was that there should be a regular levy at a low level on wealth, built on the one-off initiative that Roy Jenkins imposed. But instead of the state taking the proceeds there would be an annual payout to, say, targeted groups of the population such as those young people setting up home for the first time. Likewise, I gained no support for changing inheritance tax so that the more people you gave your wealth to, the lower would be the cumulative rate of taxation.

Failure, failure, failure every time. Yet the issue of wealth distribution will come again, and who knows how quickly there will be a push in this direction? Then the crucial judgement must be centred on ensuring the poor benefit most from any reforms on this front. Will the Old Testament law of the jubilee, which teaches of wealth being redistributed to its original owners every 50 years, be the moral imperative? Will the wealth be put into the hands of individuals or shoved into the Treasury's lockers? Having a wealth redistribution strategy that aims to reach those parts of the population that have failed to be touched by other redistribution policies constitutes an agenda that has hardly registered even among radicals, let alone socialists.

Minimum Wage

After about six years working for CPAG, I was anxious to expand the brief and my expertise. I still wanted to be an MP, but I felt strongly that as long as I worked for CPAG, who paid my wages, I should not use my position to try and gain a seat. That decision was not hard to make. No seat wanted me, such was the backlash to 'The Poor Get Poorer under Labour' campaign. Years afterwards I would be ambushed at public meetings with Labour supporters calling out that I was a Judas.

I had a responsibility to the staff which blocked me from going for other jobs that interested me. Staff salaries needed to be paid, and part of my job was to help raise the money. I was not alone, however, for CPAG was blessed in having G. R. Runciman (Lord Runciman) as its Treasurer. As well as fulfilling this role, his name acted as a bulwark against any charges that the group was a conspiracy of left-wingers trying to bring down the natural order. That was not the only value of Garry's name. He was also a superb fundraiser. In these activities, Garry was insistent at our meetings to discuss grant funding that the funds must come without strings that tied me to CPAG. But it was a consideration in my mind as the issue came up so often, and Garry had to retaliate with his ultimatum. A grant, please, with no strings, full stop. But when would I be free to move?

So I hit upon a compromise. I would develop my skills outside, but alongside, CPAG. Another newly established organization had a real attraction. It wouldn't be the same organization, going to the same donors trying to expand what was already a considerable budget necessary to cover the salaries of a large staff. Moreover, selfishly, I didn't want to have an executive to examine critically every bit of political strategy I was developing. Although I made waves on CPAG's executive, the executive always, always supported new ventures, and particularly David Bull, who would have been Director had I not applied. His behaviour to me was always exemplary. But I was an employee and subject to those conditions of my employment. I would cease to direct CPAG as soon as I became an MP. I wished to have a base from which to work, should I gain election as an MP.

CPAG dominated the benefits scene, and rightly so because it was among claimants on benefit that most poverty was to be found. However, my gut instinct told me of another issue here as well. The Abel-Smith and Townsend 1965 report *The Poor and the Poorest* highlighted the poor who were in work. But the message had somehow become lost.

I had for years been reading, in order to get up to speed on poverty, some very turgid volumes on wages councils. These were bodies that had been established to cover those industrial sectors renowned for paying desperately poor wages. Here was a weapon to fight some of the poverty wages in payment, but the machinery had fallen into disuse. Neither the employers' representatives, perhaps understandably, nor the trade union representatives, less understandably, nor the independent members, least understandably of all, had bothered to call meetings, sometimes for a decade or more. What could be done? A wages council strategy wouldn't by itself be adequate.

Many poor workers were outside their remit. But campaigning on this front would help some of the poor now and would help illustrate the need for a national strategy: i.e., a National Minimum Wage.

Philip Rowntree was the son of Seebohm Rowntree, the great instigator of poverty studies as we have come to know them. When Seebohm retired from the family chocolate factory in York, the workforce clubbed together and presented him with a sizeable cheque. Seebohm thought it wrong to spend this money on himself. Instead, he established the Seebohm Rowntree Studentship Fund, and some of that money was still unspent in 1974. Philip chaired the studentship fund. Would he set up the Low Pay Unit (LPU) I was lobbying for with this money and become our chairman? With the support of a true Rowntree daughter, Prue, and the active support of Gordon Thorpe, who had been the treasurer of the Seebohm Rowntree Studentship Fund for over 40 years, the show got on the road.

The next step required some political balancing. Philip, our major trustee, and David Layton, who had established Income Data Services, a body that collected data on wage and salary movements, were lifelong classical liberals who were very unsure about interfering on a major scale with the price paid in the labour market. It was not an idea that they immediately felt was either safe or desirable. Therefore the strategy to move to, and implement, a National Minimum Wage was carefully detailed and debated between us. But back a minimum wage campaign they did, and once the decision was agreed by them, there was never any hint of backsliding. Caution, yes, and caution over the level at which any minimum wage should be set, and how it should be reviewed and what other factors needed to be taken into account when a review was made, but total support was always forthcoming from Low Pay Unit trustees. And that support was necessary.

In today's world it would be difficult for most readers to think of Britain without a statutory minimum wage. But when we began campaigning, practically everyone was against it: the Labour Party, the Parliamentary Labour Party, the TUC and all trade unions along with, of course, the Tories and the Liberals (as the Liberal Democrats were then called). Only the National Union of Public Employees (NUPE), with its two inspirational leaders, first Alan Fisher and then Rodney Bickerstaffe, fought against this tide of reaction. These two trade union leaders represented many low-paid workers. They were fully aware of the limitations of traditional trade union action alone to win a major step change in the relative pay of the poorest workers, who were overwhelmingly women. They believed that a statutory minimum wage was necessary to make a marked difference in the lives of their members. We joined them in whatever action they were developing over our National Minimum Wage campaign.

It would be a shock to most radicals to recall the mixture of hatred and contempt that practically the whole labour movement showed to us as we tried as best we could to seek every opportunity to raise the issue of low pay, and the need for a National Minimum Wage to deal effectively with this evil. So why the hell were we interfering in the Labour movement's sphere of influence and, worse still, why did we dare to do so with such a dangerous proposal? Labour's view was supported by the classical economists, such as Milton Friedman and Friedrich Hayek. This conventional wisdom then went publicly unchallenged except by the Low Pay Unit and Unison's predecessor body. Minimum wages would cause unemployment. There was simply no doubt about that. It would also cause inflation, as workers just above the minimum wage struggled to re-establish the time-honoured differential between themselves and the poorest workers. Alan Fisher, Rodney Bickerstaffe and the Low Pay Unit were the only ones swimming against this tide.

One of my many blessings has been the gift of working with talented staff. The Low Pay Unit, which was set up in 1974, was no exception and slowly but surely we turned the wages council from a piece of machinery that might as well have been presided over by a Miss Havisham into a force for change. Wages went up, but unemployment in these sectors didn't. David Layton's organization, Incomes Data Services, carefully monitored the impact of our work in wages council areas so that we could reassure others that unemployment didn't automatically follow increases in very low pay. We also established what would now be considered a pretty obvious point, that living standards could rise independently of pay.

One of the staff at the Low Pay Unit from 1975 to 1979 was Chris Pond, who later became a Labour MP. He developed the Unit's work to cover taxation. It was another string to our bow. And it was a bow we were willing to give to others to use. On a key occasion Chris and I met the Labour backbench committee on taxation. We suggested that tax allowances, which decide the tax-free income and therefore the point at which income tax is levied, should be indexed with inflation. Up to this point, believe it or not, they hadn't been, so each year more and more low-paid workers were brought into paying tax, and the total tax burden on the low-paid increased. Jeff Rooker and Audrey Wise were present at the meeting. Andrew Bennett wasn't, though he became a crucial ally from its backbenches in helping to outmanoeuvre the Labour government. The Low Pay Unit proposed indexing allowances, and that they should remain indexed unless Parliament decided otherwise. Both Jeff and Audrey had the sheer guts and courage to compel a Labour government to adopt this strategy. It became known rightly as the Rooker–Wise Amendment. This reform is now so much part of the fiscal furniture that few will realize the courage that Jeff and Audrey had to display to make a real difference to the poor's income by lowering their tax bill. But it was the Low Pay Unit that gave Audrey and Jeff the ammunition to win this important battle to increase the poor's standard of living independently of the rewards they earned.

Making tax allowances favourable to the poor would increase their income. Here was an important lesson. Incomes could be increased in other ways than by increasing wages and child benefit. What wages and benefits will buy is dependent on prices. Lidl, Aldi, B&M and other low-cost supermarkets have been effective agents in increasing living standards in areas where they operate, as has collective bargaining. Opening up one or more of these stores in poorer areas has the same effect as giving someone a pay rise: the money they have in their hand buys more in the store and, as a result, their standard of living is increased. The social and economic impact of Lidl and Aldi on raising the poor's standard of living, which is different from the actual money that they have and therefore whether they fall on one side or other of the poverty line, has yet to provoke any serious debate. What part have these stores played in relative social peace during a time of falling real wages? Price levels and tax changes can increase the income of the poor; the most effective and obvious way of doing so is of course by increasing wage levels, although we need to be ever vigilant for any unemployment consequences for minimum wage rises.

The Low Pay Unit undertook the sheer slog of persuading individual trade union leaders, and union conferences, together with key Labour constituency parties and thereby, finally, the Labour Party conference that the one big move that could universally increase the living standards of poorer workers was the National Minimum Wage. Slowly, bloodily but surely that conference-based resolution warfare was won, and Labour began to pick up interest and then give a commitment to introduce a National Minimum Wage.

Labour's National Minimum Wage has been built on by the George Osborne initiative of introducing a National Living Wage – lower, of course, than what the campaigners for the National Living Wage want but a very significant step forward in countering the evil of low pay. It has not resulted in unemployment, but one of the unknown unknowns, to use Donald Rumsfeld's phrase, has been I believe, a stimulus, to the gig economy.

8

Social Justice: Hunger, Modern Slavery, Cool Earth

Hunger

While the causes of hunger in this country have changed, that is little comfort to those of our fellow citizens who have empty bellies as you, dear reader, read and digest this text.

The scene is a report from a worker at an evening feeding station in Birkenhead. A grandfather brought a little boy who must have been under two years old. He was carried inside his grandfather's overcoat, and the local volunteer reported:

> As we fed the little boy, his mouth opened and closed like a little bird in a nest crying out for food. I fed him with mashed shepherd's pie, teaspoonful by teaspoonful. The grandfather was embarrassed as the little boy was obviously hungry. 'He's had his tea,' the grandfather kept retorting. I said, 'We'll now have cake'. The little bird-like mouth turned to squeak 'Cake, cake, cake'. And so it was. The little boy took his fill from a beautiful cake donated to Feeding Birkenhead.

It is this story, and so many others like it, that changed my politics and political agenda. Countering hunger came to dominate my political life to a degree that I could not have imagined when I first became an MP. And this hunger is in a country with a welfare state. How can one read of this heartbreaking story of a little boy brought in his grandfather's none too warm overcoat in the middle of winter, and not be filled with compassion and charged with anger that any human being could be deliberately reduced to this condition in the sixth largest economy on earth?

So much of my politics became concentrated not simply on the poor, as my politics has always been, but on the hunger and destitution into which so many people in Britain are now thrown. It is not that I was unbothered about other issues. I was, of course, concerned. I established, for example, a multi-academy trust, and, I was equally active in campaigning against modern slavery. But I increasingly see that broader political agenda of exploitation and injustice through the lens that has spied the rise and growing dominance of hunger.

I asked David Cameron at Prime Minister's Questions back in May 2012 to prevent from becoming a reality the Trussell Trust's then estimate that the number of food bank users would double to 500,000 by the 2015 election. His teeth went around his mouth, so to speak, as he attempted to find an answer. My fault. I should have briefed him that I would ask him that question if the Speaker called me in extra time of Prime Minister's Questions.

Letter upon letter to David Cameron went unanswered when it came to action. The result: a few colleagues in the House of Commons, and I, with the help of Andrew Forsey, who then headed my House of Commons office, set up an all-party group to counter hunger. Without Andrew there would have been no sustained campaign. This national campaign gained traction with the help of the archbishop of Canterbury through having as a co-chair on our inquiry into hunger the then bishop of Truro, Tim Thornton. We then set up Feeding Britain, a national charity and possibly the first charity ever established solely by MPs and peers. Our first report in 2014 was entitled 'A Strategy for Zero Hunger in England, Wales, Scotland and Northern Ireland'.

In 2017 another report by an all-party inquiry, 'Hungry Holidays', was delivered. Its central recommendations were to legislate a national programme for all children at risk of hunger across England. Andrew Forsey and I took it upon ourselves to draft that legislation as a backbench bill and to lobby for it. One person at the end of our lobbying was Nadhim Zahawi, who was then children's minister.

The government made time for this private members' bill and announced £2 million would be allocated for a 2018 summer holiday programme. There was also a further promise of an additional £9 million in 2019. In 2020 the government made a commitment of £200 million towards an England-wide roll-out of this programme, which protected more than 600,000 children from hunger.

I had only once been in the food bank in Birkenhead. Across the shelves my eyes caught those of a constituent. The contact was momentary. Her head immediately bowed as she continued her shopping, taking stock of the contents of her food parcel. But that glance said everything. 'Do you not think it is shameful enough to be here without my MP watching me?' That look is never forgotten, however. How could I help to prevent my constituents feeling so ashamed by gaining help in a more acceptable way, while at the same time helping bring about a country free of hunger?

There was an immediate answer, and we tried to develop it in Birkenhead through our citizens' supermarket and on-site café (called Number 7). This was part of the broader Feeding Birkenhead programme, consisting of meals and activities in school holidays, as well as intensive support to ensure people claimed their full benefits entitlement so as to help also to bring their debts down to a more manageable level. But in the longer run, and just as importantly, the government must make good its failure to fully index the benefits for poorer families.

Number 7's citizens' supermarket provides people with the best-quality food for something like a third of the price they would pay in supermarkets. To try and protect members of the supermarket from any stigma, the citizens' supermarket and café share a common entrance so that no one can tell from the outside which person is going in to use which service. Once inside the shop, those with membership gain entrance to the supermarket. Everyone coming through the door can use the café even if they are not members, but membership allows purchases from the café's menu at half the price.

From Number 7 a Pink Box campaign is run which seeks to eradicate period poverty by distributing free sanitary products. Pink boxes are in junior and senior schools throughout Birkenhead where a request has been made for them – which is most of them – and in some GP centres, youth clubs and similar venues.

Number 7 also saw the 'birth' of the Baby Basics initiative with Wirral's Baby Baskets, begun with Meghan, the Duchess of Sussex, presenting the first baby basket to a hard-pressed mum. We had received reports that some mothers did not take their children to the first, and often crucial, medical check-up after birth as they could not dress their children well and feared their children would be taken into care. The baby baskets, which are full of good things for the baby and mother, come packed in Moses baskets that have within them a mattress providing the baby with their first safe sleeping quarters.

Even with the Feeding Birkenhead programme helping to prevent at least some of my constituents having to use a food bank, regular tales of desperation came to the fore. Ema Wilkes, from Neo Community, reported one family coming into their café and social supermarket which, like Number 7, provides food at a lower cost than a regular supermarket. The previous year the family bought gifts for the poorest of families. The following year they were desperately hungry. The father had lost his job. The family were quickly fed. The little boy in the family was then taken to a shelf to choose a toy. On that shelf were also baskets of food. The little boy chose the food.

After the family had been fed, the father explained they had had a bonus earlier that week. A neighbour, who was attending a funeral, had arranged that they should go to eat all the food left over from the funeral wake. But that was a few days before, and hunger had struck this family again.

On another occasion a mother who was suffering from cancer had lowered her son into a supermarket waste bin, where there was broken glass, for him to scavenge for out-of-date food. It was Christmastide, as this mother raised her son from the waste bin.

Why are there such wicked extremes of hunger, on the one hand, and concentrations of wealth of mind-boggling proportions, on the other, in Britain today?

There are two main causes, apart from the historic unequal distribution of wealth and income in this country. The first cause comes in the wake of globalization. The immediate impact of globalization in this country was to give us cheaper goods. But this was at a huge cost of stripping out most manufacturing jobs in Britain. These jobs had formed the cornerstone of an economy where wages began to meet a family's need. I firmly believe that what I witnessed over four decades in Birkenhead was the disenfranchisement of armies of semi-skilled and unskilled male workers in providing a family's income. The loss of family wage jobs has, I believe, led to an unprecedented break-up of the traditional family of two parents nurturing and caring for children — a model that has been the norm for a century or more. We also had at this time a social security system that paid proportionately more for single-parent families than it did for two-parent families. This also helped to bring about the break-up of families, or at least prevented them from being formed in the first place.

And who can blame the parents involved? They lived in an age when Mrs Thatcher preached market economics and that all of us respond to economic incentives. They responded well enough to those incentives, and as a consequence the country has seen a significant increase in the number of non-working poor families.

In the place of jobs paying family wages for so many in Birkenhead, and all parts of the country, has come employment in the gig economy, characterized by low pay, zero-hours contracts and bogus self-employment. Andrew Forsey and I made these trends in the labour market an important part of our campaigns against poverty. With the loss of jobs paying family wages all too many fathers were made irrelevant. They could no longer have sufficient income from work for this to become the cornerstone of family finances. And if on benefit, the family was disadvantaged in comparison with a family where the father had 'disappeared'. We all know the pattern, and children were and remain the great losers.

George Osborne launched a counter-attack on the most grotesque side of globalization – the payment of poverty wages – by introducing a National Living Wage. (For the background to Labour's policy of a statutory National Minimum Wage see Chapter 7.)

Poverty wages constitute the weak underbelly of a low-paying British economy. Osborne's move, sadly, came only after permanent damage had been done to the social ecology of two-parent families in which children are best nurtured. But his introduction of a National Living Wage made remarkable increases in the real wages of the poorest workers and it has not caused an increase in unemployment. That being said, it may have had the unforeseen consequence of encouraging some bosses to find new ways of circumventing this basic obligation to their workforce, through the rise of the gig economy. Here we see the greed of some of the owners of the new platform companies defining their workers as self-employed so that they, as employers, do not incur the normal labour costs of national insurance and pension contributions, not to mention Osborne's National Living Wage.

The second and now the major, and growing, driver of hunger in this country was the deliberate programme of the Cameron government of 2010 to 2015, continued by the May and Johnson governments, to cut the real value of benefit income of working-class and lower middle-class families. These cuts are now the cause of ever greater poverty and hunger in Britain.

In 2010 benefits were limited to a 1 per cent increase and there were various caps and cash ceilings placed on what claimants could receive. Then a four-year benefit freeze was introduced. Over these years families with children saw their benefits paid at around £1,800 a year lower than what they would have received if the freezes and cuts had not occurred. Over the decade from 2010, these 'reforms' resulted in the welfare state being shrunk to the tune of £37 billion.

Here is a perfectly designed strategy to reintroduce hunger on a significant scale into our country. And hunger has been the result. Ministers may have been muddle-headed when discussing the impact of such significant changes. They may not have thought through what the consequences would be of attacking the living standards of the poorest people in Britain by preventing benefits matching price inflation.

If this policy, which has had such evil outcomes, was not understood by ministers, then it shows a lack of intelligence on their part, or how distant their lives are from the precariousness of the living standards of so many of their constituents. Whatever the cause, hunger has been the outcome, and it is the outcome of actions, and lack of subsequent action, taken by those men and women who have sat around the Cabinet table since the strategy was approved and implemented, and who have made no move to be regularly informed of the outcome of that strategy and then act to counter it. As part of the counter-Covid economic measures the Chancellor, Rishi Sunak, increased the universal credit level by £1,000 for each eligible household. The result? Shorter queues outside food banks. This move to counter poverty is now abolished, and with its abolition have come significantly longer queues outside food banks.

If we are to put an end to the shame felt by people who are hungry and seek help, like my constituent who saw me in the food bank, the benefit cuts must be reversed for all benefits, and quickly. And we urgently need to support the development of social or citizens' supermarkets of the type being developed by Feeding Britain so that hungry people can receive food and advice as part of a dignified service.

Up until the Covid rise in expenditure there had been a significant reduction in the deficit in the government's budget. That deficit had been very largely reduced by the savings made by the cuts in benefits to our citizens who are of working age. Those above retirement age have seen their benefits increase in real terms by 3 percentage points. Working-age families have experienced a sharp drop in their living standards.

The IOU which we as the public owe the poor, who have paid most for the reduction in the government deficit, must be redeemed. We must ensure that poor families have a minimum income which provides enough for food, heating, secure and stable housing, clean clothing and all those very basic necessities to which many of us never have to give a second thought. Until that day of the jubilee arrives, Feeding Britain will continue to think up the means to help to feed the hungry and, while doing so, seek media coverage so that the maximum pressure is put on the government to act and abolish hunger.

Modern Slavery

In a Good Friday meditation in 2019 the Pope asked Sister Eugenia Bonetti, who was then 80, to reflect on her work of trying to save individuals from the clutches of modern slave owners. She did so by meditating at each of the 14 Stations of the Cross, and in so doing presented how evil human slavery was.

At the Sixth Station, where Veronica wipes the face of Jesus, Sister Eugenia invited us to 'Think of all those children in various parts of the world who cannot go to school but are instead exploited in mines, fields and fisheries, bought and sold by human traffickers for organ harvesting, used and abused on our streets by many, including Christians, who have lost the sense of their own and others' sacredness.'

At the Eleventh Station, where Jesus is nailed to the Cross, Sister Eugenia recalled:

Our society proclaims equal rights and dignity for all human beings. Yet it practises and tolerates ... extreme forms of inequality. Men, women and children are bought and sold as slaves by new traders in human lives. The victims of trafficking are then exploited by others. And in the end, they are cast aside, discarded as worthless goods. How many people are growing rich by devouring the flesh and blood of the poor?

At the Fourteenth Station, where Jesus is laid in the tomb, Sister Eugenia spoke of how

The desert and the seas have become the new cemeteries of our world. These deaths leave us speechless. Yet responsibility has to be taken. People let their brothers and sisters die: men, women, children that we could not, or would not, save. While governments closed off their palaces of power, the Sahara is filled with the bones of men and women who could not survive exhaustion, hunger and thirst. How much pain is involved in these new exoduses? How much cruelty is inflicted on those fleeing their homelands: in their desperate journeys, in the extortion and tortures they endure, in the sea that becomes a watery grave?[*]

In my campaigning against modern slavery, a Providential blessing was at work. Patrick White, who then headed my parliamentary office, decided I should accept the invitation to speak at the launch of the Centre for Social Justice's

[*]Sister Eugenia Bonetti, 'Meditations: With Christ and With Women on the Way of the Cross', Rome, April 2019.

report 'It Happens Here: Equipping the United Kingdom to Fight Modern Slavery'. I was not so keen on going. I knew nothing about the subject. But you do not argue with Patrick, just as you don't argue with Andrew Forsey, who held that position after Patrick. Both of these have accidentally proved further providential blessings.

The room was full of organizations whose purpose was to rescue and support victims of modern slavery. Hundreds of people were present. The press conference went on for far, far too long. Four or five speakers had been billed. I was last in this line of succession, so to speak. My bones ached with – dare I say? – the boredom that comes from speeches that are too long. What could I say? I decided to get up and beg for 30 seconds more of the audience's time. I said that we needed to call slavery what it was, not just trafficking, which can make it sound like the stuff of a trade association. We must call it slavery. And, I said, we need a Modern Slavery Act to change the world in the way Wilberforce had done. The room exploded with applause – whether for the idea of a new slavery act or for the release in 30 seconds I knew not.

I spent that summer with a member of staff, Tim Weedon, lobbying Fiona Hill, the then political adviser to Theresa May (the then Home Secretary) for a new slavery bill. Coffee after coffee was drunk. Meeting after meeting was concluded with the project, I thought, going nowhere. Then, suddenly, Fiona told us that the lobbying had been successful, and Mrs May was interested in a bill. I chaired the scoping inquiry on what that bill should contain and then the joint select committee of both Lords and Commons considering the draft bill.

I still don't know what was in Fiona's mind. Why did it take so long on an issue crying out for justice, and one that would play well in Mrs May's leadership election, which would at some point engulf the Tory Party? Why was success granted at the stage it was? And what had been the barrier to advancing this great cause? On the day that Fiona reported the Home Secretary would commit to a bill, I had been asked by Fiona what organization would undertake the lead-up to the Bill. I replied that I thought the organization which would do this was obvious: it should be the Centre for Social Justice (CSJ), which had initiated the report that had captured my imagination on the urgency of the task to counter modern slavery. It was, however, at the mention of the CSJ that Fiona's attitude changed in favour of the bill. That change seemed to occur in a moment, in the twinkling of an eye.

We had passed the first step to making an effective strategy against modern slavery and all the horrors that it involves. During our scoping exercise, the members of the commission, Baroness Elizabeth Butler-Sloss, Sir John (now Lord) Randall, and I, listened to the testimony of slaves.

I have still not recovered from hearing and witnessing those sessions, so what must the impact be on the lives of those who have experienced at first hand the deadly evil of slavery? Most, but not all, of those giving evidence were female victims, and they were invariably women of colour. They quietly told us, in broken English or through interpreters, the hell that had broken practically every part of their humanity except that most basic of our drives – the determination to survive.

Most victims did not sob. Yet the eyes of each of them shed tears as their voices quietly told of the hideousness and terror they had been through. Time and time again, both during these sessions and ever since, I've wondered if anyone could recover to become anything like whole again once they had escaped the evil and villainous clutches of the slave owner? In writing that phrase, I know how inadequate today's language is to describe the sinfulness and wickedness of the organizers of modern slavery.

My mind has never settled since I began that first scoping inquiry and met with people who had escaped slavery. I was puzzled then, and am more puzzled now, as to why this issue gained so little traction with the public. How could there have been so little political response from the media, who play such an important role in awakening the conscience of a large section of the nation, when horrific injustices are happening around us in our own country?

Of all the campaigns with which I have been involved, not being able to help awaken and fire the national outrage at the growth and existence of modern-day slavery must count as one of my biggest failures. There was, of course, much response from those dedicated individuals from voluntary bodies who were freeing slaves from bondage. But here we are preaching to the converted. There was no stirring of that great national consciousness that is crucial for helping to drive every reform with which I've been associated.

There was, though, thank God, a response from Theresa May. Yet on two counts, both in the scoping inquiry and the joint select committee of both Houses, the most radical of proposals met with immediate failure. First was the lack of compassion that should be given to protecting people who have escaped somehow or other from slavery. We won changes to the level and duration of care the government was prepared to give to people who had escaped slavery – but given the enormity of the crime, these concessions were pretty thin.

I met Sister Eugenia, who was asked by the Pope to give those Good Friday reflections on modern slavery, when I was in Rome at a conference called by the Pope on how best to counter modern slavery. Here I also met groups of sisters whose lives were devoted to providing help, cover and escape for victims of modern slavery. You couldn't talk to a single sister, let alone all 25 or so of them, without realizing that a network of safe houses for those escaping slavery was crucial. More, these victims of slavery need love, lots of love, and the security that comes from unconditional love, if they are to begin a life of recovery. Religious orders are particularly well placed to give this unconditional love. But the sisters, working across religious boundaries, and defying the culture of Pope John Paul's hard line, knew that the fishing nets that try and catch the victims of modern slavery have huge gaps within them and that many victims of slavery are left, all too often, to fend for themselves. Soon many of them are recaptured or, in their utter loneliness and pennilessness, re-subject themselves to their slave-master.

Most of the slavery that benefits practically all of us in this country is imported, not through human cargoes but through supply chains of those businesses and services on which we greatly depend. We won a paper victory in including in the Act the need for commercial organizations with annual turnovers of £36 million or more to present in their annual accounts what, if anything, they've done to eliminate slavery from their supply chains. This was a paper victory, but paper victories can have long-term importance. Once it had been accepted by Theresa May and the then Prime Minister, David Cameron, that business had such an obligation to report, even if they had done nothing to safeguard their supply chains, we gained for a later stage of our campaign that crucial foothold that the reform should be made more effective. A very important lesson here for reformers is that, once the desirability of a reform is conceded, it is much easier to build on those modest beginnings than to establish the new bridgehead. Since then, I have met with those people offering a golden standard of care that we should aim to give to all those rescued from slavery. Putting pressure on the supply chains of organizations is the next step in our campaign. Also I campaigned so that the Speakers of the House of Commons and House of Lords established a joint committee to study how much slavery is hidden in supply chains for those goods and services supplied to Parliament.

As a result of that collective action, we now have a Modern Slavery Act. Recently the then Home Secretary, Sajid Javid, and the then Prime Minister, Theresa May, asked Maria Miller MP, Baroness Butler-Sloss and me, as chair, to review the workings of the Act and to report what changes must be made for us to make far better inroads into countering this most wicked trade. Our proposals are still being implemented; and so the fight goes on.

Cool Earth

I came late to environmental campaigning. I knew the dangers of global heating and the importance of rainforests as being one of the most important, if not *the* most important, bulwark against what seems to be the inexorable rise in global temperatures. But I did little about it until one day in 2005 I saw a photograph in the *Times* of part of the Brazilian rainforest owned by Johan Eliasch, a Swedish businessman who is CEO of the sports brand Head.

The caption under the photograph talked of the millions of acres that Johan was helping to preserve. I immediately emailed him and asked whether he would be interested in establishing a rainforest campaign. He impressed me greatly by immediately emailing a reply. Johan suggested we should talk. We did.

There are a lot of rainforest charities, Johan warned me. 'Save the Rainforest' was a well-worn slogan more associated with failure than success. But I made the point that, while he was able to protect millions of rainforest trees, others of us might wish to join in a campaign that would match his efforts. Cool Earth (Johan's choice of name) was born.

The only other question of substance that he asked me was who I thought could lead such an organization. I immediately replied Matthew Owen, and the rest is history. It is under Matthew's stewardship that Cool Earth has led the way in putting funds and power with the people who live in the rainforest.

I have helped add two aspects in the development of the organization's strategy. I was keen that the funding should go towards building a firewall that would help prevent loggers, ranchers and miners gaining access to the heart of the rainforest. This would be done by ensuring the ownership of forest on the firewall would be owned by local communities themselves.

This 'firewall' strategy resulted in more rainforest being protected from destruction than can be claimed by any government or non-governmental organization. As Cool Earth never fails to remind me, there is only one group with a real track record of keeping the forest standing. It's not governments, the UN, World Bank or the green movement. It's indigenous people and local communities.

The future of Cool Earth will partly lie in a strategy whereby money goes to local people who themselves decide how to spend it. Judging by Cool Earth's experience this will lead not only to the best protection ever of existing rainforest but also to a social economic reform directed at health and educational needs.

Cool Earth's strategy is a renunciation of the World Bank's top-down policy whereby large sums of money are held by the World Bank to counter rainforest destruction. Much is spent on holding international conferences and seminars, but little multilateral funding to counter rainforest destruction goes to support those people who have for generations known how best to farm these crucial areas.

I'd also been interested at the same time in trying to see advances made by the Commonwealth. Here is the second part of my contribution to Cool Earth. I found it almost unintelligible that the Tory Party, in particular, could go into general elections without even a mention of the Commonwealth, let alone detailed proposals of how to ensure the survival and development of this crucial organization. Commonwealth countries make up over 20 per cent of the world's total land mass and amount to almost a third of the world's population.

How much rainforest exists in the Commonwealth was a question I put to Matthew Owen. He immediately told me that no Commonwealth country, with only a few exceptions (notably Papua New Guinea and Canada), had very substantial holdings. He would go away and research how large the collective Commonwealth ownership was of this vital world survival plantation. He reported back that collectively the Commonwealth had the second-largest holding after Brazil. Here was the birth of the Queen's Commonwealth Canopy.

There was also a demonstration of how self-interested altruism could work. If the Commonwealth began to realize its importance as a protector of rainforest, then Commonwealth leaders would have an international role in developing a strategy of rainforest survival. There could also be important jobs available in developing this strategy for some Commonwealth leaders, but would Commonwealth countries respond?

The idea of the Queen's Commonwealth Canopy was to be the first step in a strategy that would rebuild Commonwealth politics. Instead of being largely a ceremonial organization, it would be one that promoted Commonwealth objectives.

The aim of initiating the Queen's Commonwealth Canopy was to begin these new politics. The original aim was for each Commonwealth country either to commit some of its existing rainforest as part of the Queen's Canopy or, if it had no forest, for it to finance preservation in other Commonwealth countries. The success now stands with every Commonwealth country participating as a member of the canopy. What has not developed, sadly, is the Commonwealth looking at other issues where, if joined together, it could collectively be a major player in world politics. That era is to come.

During the initial publicity over the Queen's Commonwealth Canopy, individuals in this country wrote to ask whether they could be members by planting trees. They couldn't. This idea of home planting developed into an initiative as the Queen's Green Canopy to celebrate the late Queen Elizabeth's Platinum Jubilee. Plant a tree for the Jubilee, as the then Prince of Wales suggested, became a major part of the Queen's Platinum Jubilee celebrations. So far, this campaign has been responsible in this country for the planting of over a million trees.

Cool Earth has been an example of a proactive campaign with people who live in rainforests to protect the best bulwark against global warming. This has also tried to initiate new Commonwealth politics. Likewise, it is now a player in Britain itself in trying to plant trees as a counter-attack against global warming.

9

Preventing Poor Children from Becoming Poor Adults: Early Years, Parenting, Schools

Shortly after winning the 2010 general election David Cameron, the new Prime Minister, asked me to head an Independent Review on Poverty and Life Chances. His aims for the Review were to generate a broader debate about the nature and extent of poverty in the UK, examine the case for changing the way poverty is measured, explore how a child's home environment affects their chances of being ready to take full advantage of their schooling and recommend action by government and other institutions to reduce poverty and enhance life chances for the least advantaged, consistent with the government's fiscal strategy.

What I wrote for the Review reflected how my ideas on combatting poverty have developed over the last five decades – the first decade was spent at the Child Poverty Action Group and the four subsequent decades representing Birkenhead in the House of Commons. As a result, I have come to view poverty as a much more subtle enemy than purely lack of money, and I have similarly become increasingly concerned about how the poverty that parents endure is all too often visited on their children to such a degree that they continue to be poor as they enter adulthood.

A new body of research has shown that, while income is still important, it is not the exclusive or necessarily the dominant cause of poverty being handed on from one generation to another. The fact that the home learning environment and the quality of childcare are so important in deciding the fate of children means that we have to change tack. Let me start at the beginning.

The traditional approach to defining poverty (which the 2010 Child Poverty Act enshrined in law), has its roots in the work of Charles Booth and Seebohm Rowntree over 140 years ago. Rowntree, who gave precision to this approach, was specifically concerned with determining what sum of money would allow families to achieve a minimum standard of living. Families below this level of income were deemed to be poor; those above it were not. In calculating the number of poor families, Rowntree made a distinction between those households who simply did not have enough money to meet his minimum living standard, and so ward off poverty, and those families whose income could achieve this standard but who decided to spend part of their income in other ways.

The 2010 Child Poverty Act was the culmination of one of the most audacious and welcome initiatives of the last Labour government. Keeping hold of Rowntree's approach to defining poverty in money terms had important advantages. A political consensus emerged across all parties to pass the 2010 Act. The heightened political importance given to countering child poverty was thankfully matched by action, with vastly more funding redistributed to families in need.

Why, then, was I the only Member of Parliament to caution against the Act? I believed that the results of this strategy were more modest than taxpayers hoped for, especially considering the huge sums involved. More worrying still, the stubbornly obstinate number of children in poverty showed that this strategy had stalled even before the years of austerity. I further believed that the Act was in danger of closing down a debate on alternative means of reaching the goal, when a wider debate on alternative strategies was precisely what was most needed.

I did not express my concerns about the Bill because I had in any way changed the degree of importance I attached to combating monetary poverty. It was, rather, that I no longer believed that the strategy of concentrating alone on income transfers could achieve the goal of abolishing child poverty by 2020, as Tony Blair had hoped, even on a crude financial measure. Nor did I believe it would break the inter-generational transfer of poverty.

One result of the 2010 Child Poverty Act was to straitjacket our understanding of poverty to one particular financial manifestation, along the lines Rowntree set out in his 1901 report. Of course, the current poverty line has been much revised to match rising incomes. But this income measure not only drives media interest, and thereby the broad understanding voters have of what the government is trying to achieve, but also, more importantly, it drives government policy in a single direction which is in danger of becoming counter-productive. The anti-poverty agenda is driven along a single track of hunting down families who live below this line and then marking up a success as a family is moved across the line, no matter how marginal is the advance in their income. It does little to concentrate on those children who endure persistent poverty. Worse still, this approach has prevented a much more comprehensive strategy from emerging on how best, in the longer run, to counter child poverty in a way that prevents poor children from becoming poor adults.

On visits to different parts of the country I have met large numbers of parents anxious to know how they can better advance the long-term interests of their children. But, as my report for Prime Minister Cameron argued, a modern definition of poverty must take into account those children whose parents remain disengaged from their responsibilities. Tesco reported in the survey they undertook for the Review that in one of their east London stores their staff defined poverty in modern Britain and had decided how best the Review could cut the supply routes to adult poverty. Tesco's employees' conclusions were a million miles away from the classical Rowntree approach. The staff reported on the changing pattern of stealing. Children were now far less inclined to steal sweets. Instead, the targets were sandwiches, to assuage their hunger, and clean underwear, which they also lacked. Does anyone any longer believe that this modern face of neglect will be countered by simple increases in Universal Credit?

I had a further consideration that went beyond the arbitrariness of the definitions put forward in the Bill, and the failing impact of the fiscal redistribution strategy. I no longer believe that the poverty endured by all too many children can simply be measured by their parents' lack of income. Something more fundamental than the scarcity of money is adversely dominating the lives of these children.

Since 1969 I have witnessed a growing indifference from some parents to meeting the most basic needs of children, and particularly younger children, those who are least able to fend for themselves. I have also observed how the home life of a minority – but, worryingly, a growing minority – of children fails to express an unconditional commitment to the successful nurturing of children.

Why do these observations matter? The most disturbing pieces of research that I have read are a handful of studies showing that the successes individuals achieve during their adult life can be predicted by the level of cognitive and non-cognitive skills they possess on their first day at school. These differences in skill levels have also been noted after as little as 22 months of life and are shown to widen in the toddler population by the age of five. Moreover, these skill levels are related to class, or, as it is now more commonly spoken of, the income of their parents. The findings also worryingly show that the brightest five-year-olds from poorer homes are overtaken by the progress of their peers from richer homes by the time they are ten.

So how do I square these findings – which directly relate the level of income of parents to their children's success – with my belief that money alone does not produce the transforming effect we need to counter child poverty at this time?

The answer, paradoxically, comes from the very studies that show how early on life's race is now determined for most children. These studies have not used class or income as a roadblock to further analysis. Instead, they try to hold class and income constant and examine the other forces at work that govern a child's life chances. Once this approach is adopted, we find that income is not the only factor that matters, and that it is not even the main one. Even if the money were available to lift all children out of income poverty in the short term, it is far from clear that this move would in itself close the achievement gap.

These studies show that there is much more beyond just improving short-term family incomes in determining the life chances of poor children. A healthy pregnancy, positive but authoritative parenting, high-quality childcare, a positive approach to learning at home and an improvement in parents' qualifications can together transform children's life chances and trump the child's class background and parental income. A child growing up in a family with these attributes has every chance of succeeding in life, even if the family is poor. Other research has shown that the simple fact of a mother or father being interested in their children's education increases a child's chances of moving out of poverty as an adult by 25 percentage points.

At the moment poor children are much less likely, on average, to benefit from these advantages. But with the right support from the government, the voluntary sector and society as a whole this doesn't always have to be true. If we can ensure that parents from poor families know how best to extend the life opportunities of their children (the advantages that many middle-class and rich families take for granted and which a significant number of working-class parents achieve), then – even if we cannot end income poverty in the short term – we can break this inter-generational cycle of disadvantage. We can ensure that poor children don't inevitably take their poverty into adulthood.

Some children from low-income families have consistently done well, but these examples are few and their experience is not common for the whole group. This is not, however, universally true in the UK. Chinese children from poor families as a group do better than all other non-poor children. Growing up in an ethnically Chinese family in England is enough to overcome all of the disadvantages of being poor. This surely has much to do with parental aspirations and attitudes. It would be a betrayal of all our children if we were to say that what this group already achieves cannot be achieved by all British children.

One of the central recommendations of the report to Prime Minister Cameron was to establish a set of life chances indicators. The research material that has disturbed me most also sounds the clearest note of hope. And it is this research work that has served as the launch pad for a set of Life Chances Indicators. This small clutch of studies shows those home attributes that need to be universalized if we are to prevent life's wheel of fortune consistently spinning against the interests of poorer children as a class. The universalism of these attributes is the sole aim of what I called in the report the Foundation Years. The success of the Foundation Years in narrowing the range of children's abilities should be measured by the Life Chances Indicators. The Review recommended that the government adopt these Indicators and use them to drive Foundation Years policy. These new Life Chances Indicators should run alongside the definitions laid out in the 2010 Child Poverty Act.

These Indicators are crucial to widening the existing narrow debate and over-emphasis on income levels. This is not a semantic point. The existing poverty measurements take a snapshot of income to see how many families have an income at or below 60 per cent of median income. The Life Chances Indicators, on the other hand, will be essential to measuring how well we are achieving what would become the primary goal of cutting the entry route that all too many poor children inexorably tread into adult poverty.

The Indicators should be a means by which the government reports annually to the electorate on how well its intention to raise the cognitive and non-cognitive skills of poorer children is working out in practice. The purpose of the indicators is not to sideline the goal of abolishing child poverty; it is, rather, to set out an alternative and broader strategy by which to achieve this goal.

The success of the approach will be to change over the longer term the distribution of income. This will not be achieved through a primary emphasis on income redistribution. The goal of changing the distribution of income will be achieved by ensuring that poorer children in the future have the range of abilities necessary to secure better-paid, higher-skilled jobs.

The Life Chances Indicators should both measure the effectiveness and drive reform of all programmes directed under the new Foundation Years strategy, in which the role of parents is central. Currently few people are able to identify how, except by provding midwives, government and the community formally support families with children aged under five. By establishing the Foundation Years – which will encapsulate all early

119

years policy — the government would be providing parents with a clear guide by which to navigate their way around what will become a series of connected and coordinated forms of support.

Establishing the Foundation Years will further help the government to communicate to the country that it intends to make a decisive move in transforming the life chances of poorer children. The government will be publicly recognizing the significance of this period of life as the base for future life achievements when it appoints a Secretary of State specifically responsible for driving this policy across government.

The Foundation Years should become the essential first part of a new tripartite system of education: the Foundation Years, leading into the School Years, leading into Further, Higher and Continuing Education.

A central assumption of the Foundation Years is that the great driving force for deciding children's future is their parents. No policy designed to break through the glass ceiling that is firmly in place over the heads of all too many children can succeed without parents. The very best that governments and communities can do is to support parents to enable them to be even more effective agents of change for their children. But there are other roles that communities and governments must play if we are radically to improve the life chances of poorer children.

The Early Years experiment in Ellesmere Port is an example of working with vulnerable mothers from their pregnancy onwards. The project offers support to pregnant young mothers and to other mothers who find it most difficult to nurture their children without help. The group is largely composed of pregnant mothers or mothers with young children who have not known what it is to have a good mother to teach them the skills to nurture their children. The aim of the project is to narrow the skills gap between the most disadvantaged children and other children before they begin school.

In the early 1950s the anthropologist Geoffrey Gorer noted that the spread of a 'tough love' style of parenting had been the agent that changed England from a centuries-long tradition of brutality into what was described by visitors to these shores in the late nineteenth and early twentieth centuries as one of the most peaceful European nations. The 'tough love' tradition of parenting did more than turn England into what was until recently a peaceful, self-governing kingdom. Research published much more recently on different kinds of parenting shows that the style most beneficial to a child's emotional and intellectual development is this particular style of nurturing. But that 'tough love' tradition has recently been in retreat.

There are several reasons why Britain is witnessing a rupturing in its once strong parenting tradition. Very few sets of secular ideas are not revised or replaced by succeeding generations. The growth of a 'tough love' approach was bound to inspire detractors as a wider movement took hold questioning established hierarchies, whether those hierarchies were within families or within society more widely.

Post-war housing policy has also enjoyed more than a walk-on role. Mega developments, sweeping up communities, shaking them around and scattering them onto new estates, often on the periphery of the towns where they had long-established roots, also played a major part in the break-up of the extended, matriarchal family hierarchy, and in so doing destroyed the support that this informal network provided for couples as they began the process of starting a family.

Other powerful forces were also at work. Our country's de-industrialization destroyed more than the work ethic in many families and communities. The major means by which many males were socialized into wider society was lost, as was their role as breadwinners. Bob Rowthorn, the sociologist, and David Webster, the economist, reported to the Review on Foundation Years their work in establishing a link from the 1980s between a decline in male employment and the growth of single-parent families. Their thesis supports my contention that governments should have put much more of their energy in getting young males into work, rather than over-zealously pressurizing single mothers to enter the labour market.

The story does not end here. The sociologist Norman Dennis reminded the Review that communities have insisted from time immemorial that men who beget children should be made to support those children and the children's mother, usually by marriage. But in a fit of what at best can be charitably described as absent-mindedness, or as not wishing to cause a fuss, a whole number of governments forgot that one of its primary duties in safeguarding the well-being of children is to enforce the father's financial responsibility. Children have been the clear losers, and it has not gone unnoticed by them.

Some time ago I asked to meet a group of 15-year-old pupils in one of Birkenhead's most challenged schools – so that I could talk to them about their school contracts. I asked each of them to list which six outcomes they most wanted to gain for themselves from attending school. Their replies both shocked and delighted me. Without exception, all of these young citizens stated that they wanted their school to be a safe place, to help teach them what was involved in building long-term friendships and to equip them with the necessary skills to gain a good job. Most surprisingly, all of the pupils listed as one as their remaining requests the wish to be taught how to be good parents.

After talking with this group of young people the headteacher remarked that perhaps ten out of the group of 25 had rarely, if ever, known their parents to put their needs before their own. Yet none of these young people judged their parents – they phrased their request as wishing to know how to be good parents. Some of the group were scruffy, their clothes washed less often than those of other children, and apart from school dinners they had no certainty when they would next be fed. Where they would sleep that night was similarly problematic for some of that group. Would they gain entrance when they went home, or would tonight again be spent on the floor of a friend's home?

These young, vulnerable but eager constituents battled against home circumstances that would probably have broken me, and yet they prioritized the need to know how to be good parents, not simply better parents than the ones they had inherited.

Some time later I went to visit a new Academy in Manchester. I again met a group of 15-year-old pupils, to whom I set the same task. All of the pupils similarly wanted to know how to become good parents, and saw offering guidance on this as one of the six responsibilities they wished their school to fulfil. Here is the basis for the report's key recommendation that we should seek ways of teaching parenting and life skills through the existing national curriculum, with appropriate modules being available for study through a range of existing subjects.

Compare the current belief that parenting is taught by a process of osmosis with the education the state insists that those wishing to adopt children must undergo. Six major areas of study have to be undertaken, and this is the training of adults who want to care for children.

Raising knowledge about parenting skills within the school curriculum is the first critical move to change the direction of the tide from what has been the long retreat from the 'tough love' style of parenting.

Richard Layard and John Coleman, both pioneers in promoting happiness as an objective, stressed to the Review that those skills in parenting and life skills need to be developed and not dismissed as being soft; they have important, hard-edged outcomes. If we are truly to bring about a once-in-a-generation cultural shift, we will need to think at every level of society about how all of us can support individuals, families and communities giving greater value to, and then active support emphasizing, the importance of parenting.

The second place in life's natural journey where governments can emphasize the importance the whole society attaches to parenting could be in natal and post-natal classes. These courses should be expanded from the all too common concentration on the birth process to a revision of the GCSE material covering child development and the practice by which parents can broaden the life chances of their children.

Reading is important also. In addition to building their children's self-confidence, the guide cites reading to children as one of the most important activities parents can undertake in increasing their skills and advancing their children's life chances. And while reading is only one part of the home environment's influence, I believe that a virtuous circle can be built by improving the bonding with children that takes place when reading with them, and the confidence that parents themselves gain.

Given a fair wind, we may be at one of those rare moments when a decisive change could occur in both the nation's attitude to the great responsibilities of parenting and in the resolve of individual parents. We need to establish five-star parenting courses, with the courses coming from the distillation of the community's collective wisdom. It will embolden many parents to practise the good parenting guide and so help a snowball effect that changes the whole climate of options.

I do not believe that we can make the Foundation Years the success they must become without Sure Start. But the concept of the Sure Start Children's Centre needs radical reform. Sure Start initially aimed at equalizing life chances before children started school. It was converted to a Job Centre service to get mothers into work. To focus Sure Start's resources on narrowing those differences in children's abilities requires turning what has become today's Sure Start model upside down, reverting to the original vision that David Blunkett had of providing greatest help to the most disadvantaged. However, reform must avoid the risk of Sure Start becoming simply a service for poorer families.

Decreasing class-based differences with which children currently arrive at school should be put at the centre of every Sure Start children's centre contract, and the contract should clearly link payments to outcomes against this benchmark.

I asked the headmaster of Bidston Avenue Primary School in Birkenhead if he and his staff would list the skills they believed all children should posess as they start school. The skills the head listed as those which a significant number of children lack when they start school were: to be able to sit still and listen; to be aware of other children; to understand the word No, and the borders it sets for behaviour, and equally to understand the word Stop, and that such a phrase might be used to prevent danger; to be potty-trained and able to go to the loo; to recognize their own name; to speak to an adult to ask for needs; to be able to take off their coat and tie up laces; to talk in sentences; and to be able to open and enjoy a book.

On every visit I have carried out I have asked parents how they would change their Sure Start. All parents without exception praised Sure Start. All parents, however, again without exception, said that if they were running 'their' centres there would be activities after 3.30, at weekends and especially during the school holidays. Some parents noticed how their children lost skills during school holidays, and particularly the long summer break. They were all in favour of sensibly staging holidays throughout the school years. Here are a number of issues that will need to be addressed if more progress is to be made during the school years in improving the life chances of poor children.

The best way of achieving these changes is for parents with children in the Foundation Years to become involved in the new governance of Sure Start Mark II, and by taking seats on the board.

Sure Start should aim to become centres of world renown, breaking down the rigid division between paid professional help and volunteers. Health visitors must become the key workers, undertaking the complex work needed to engage and support the most vulnerable families. They also need to build up teams of other professional workers to oversee a new cadre of volunteers to access the homes where children are currently not being reached. Similarly, midwives should be encouraged to build up a small volunteer team to support mothers wishing to breastfeed, who will be at the end of the telephone to help breastfeeding mothers at any time during the day or night.

The success of parents in nurturing their children goes far beyond the range of abilities their children possess and how well these talents may be developed. The impact goes even beyond forming the basis of a more peaceful and self-governing society. It helps to determine the overall prosperity of the country.

Reform in improving the educational outcomes of children has not kept pace with the demands our economy now puts on its labour force. Britain's destiny, now more than ever, is dependent on our success as a trading nation, and to prosper our country needs to be a leader in the value-added stakes. This continual improvement in taking our skills upmarket has not happened, or at least not at a fast enough rate, and large numbers of young adults have been left unqualified for jobs that pay good wages.

The Review on Poverty and Life Chances located the root of this failure to ensure the country has an adequate skills base not in the school system but in those years before children go to school. To ensure that the other two pillars of education – schools and further, higher and continual education – can carry out their task well, it is crucial for a government to act as it did during the coalition administration, when it put R. A. Butler's Education Act onto the statute book in 1944, thereby kick-starting another wave of upward social mobility. A similar decisive move is now called for in establishing the Foundation Years as the first of three pillars of our education system.

There are considerable grounds for optimism. Trends in wider society are moving in a direction that supports the trust of the Foundation Years Review's proposals. The work that the sociologist Geoff Dench submitted to the Review looked at what mothers themselves think or do, rather than having their view distorted by interest groups. The circumstances that made them most happy and contented are having a husband or partner in work so that they can combine their work and their family responsibilities in a pattern that gives primacy to their families. This model, which favours the best nurturing of children, is quietly advancing. Dench's research, like that of Rowthorn and Webster, points to the importance of male employment rates to family formation and stability. Moreover, most families do not escape from poverty by working unless one member of the household works full-time.

THE CULTURE OF RESPECT

I know very well that [this country] is not a realm of unfailing virtue and goodness. That does not alter the fact that it managed to produce a form of existence which is freer of the sins against one's neighbour than any other community has attained … it excels in having come to terms with the fact that people in large numbers need both to be conscious of one another and leave one another alone.

These were the words used by a continental refugee, Sir Geoffrey Elton, to describe the Britain he had chosen to live in. They were admittedly uttered in another age, but that other age was only 1984. In this chapter I want to describe how a particular British character was shaped, one that was instrumental in bringing about the largely self-governing community described above.

Britain's long march to respectability was shaped by Christianity, the role of working-class mutuality and the place of English Idealism.

In the next chapter I shall examine those forces which I see as responsible for the Balkanization of this peaceable kingdom: a vicious meltdown in skilled and semi-skilled manual jobs and with it a sharp increase in the number of broken families and the widespread loss of parenting skills; educational reform which was beneficial to the most able of working-class children, but which left a vast majority of their peers ill equipped to hold down those decent jobs which continued to exist; a drink and drugs culture together with a social-media-driven individualistic culture that thrives at the expense of a collective or public ethic. Nor must it be forgotten how we, as a country, became careless to the point of irresponsibility in assuming that the kind of character which imbued a peaceable kingdom would continue without the most careful and continuous nurturing. Into this foul mixture of decline I do not add welfare as a prime cause of our present discontent. Welfare's role is of a different nature: it operates in a manner that reinforces and exaggerates the weakness inflicted by the other causes discussed here.

I am not so naive as to believe that those three forces which in the past once made Britain so peaceful a society can be simply reconstructed. I do see a role, however, for a new, contract culture as a means of regaining the kind of society that so attracted Sir Geoffrey Elton to Britain's shore not so many decades ago. Indeed, at the moment I do not see any option other than to embrace this approach.

10

The Ethic of Respect:
A Left-Wing Cause

There is no index by which we can measure the rise and subsequent collapse of respect, or the practice of a culture of common decency. Two sets of information give the lie to those who claim that an expression of concern at the collapse of common decencies is simply the middle class stirring up moral panic. First, the number of violent crimes against the person in Edwardian times and those actions that were deemed to be so severe a lapse from decent behaviour that they warranted imprisonment. Here are illustrations, if any are needed, of just how triumphant Britain's march towards respectability was in establishing a peaceful and largely self-governing society, and one in which the law played only a residual role.

The level of violence against the person is an index, I believe, although an extreme one, of our endemic lack of mutual respect. Of course, the different rates by the public of reporting crime have to be considered and will without any doubt account for some of the differences in the data presented. Yet the extremes of these figures cannot be wished away on technical grounds alone. Because, as the march of respectable society became a reality, crimes of violence against the person almost became extinct. In 1900 there were only 1,908 such crimes reported in the entire country. When I was an MP, there were on average more violent crimes against individuals in each parliamentary constituency in England and Wales than there were for the whole country a century ago. Indeed, violent crimes, though slowly rising through the past hundred years, began to escalate only in the 1960s, which adds a particularly unpleasant twist to the poet Philip Larkin's insight into what began in 1963. Today, sadly, such crimes have broken through the million barrier.

Here is the second set of data. The same trend can also be seen from the prison data of a little over a hundred years ago. What society defines as a crime, let alone a crime that deserves a prison sentence, changes over time and reflects, to some extent, how serious particular crimes are perceived to be. The historian Jose Harris has commented on what the Edwardians considered so serious a lapse in behaviour that it warranted imprisonment. I happily cite this evidence for those who contend that I (and others who think similarly) have simply conjured up a peaceful golden age which never existed.

Jose Harris reports that in 1912–13

one quarter of males aged 16 to 21 who were imprisoned in the Metropolitan area of London were serving seven-day sentences for offences which included drunkenness, playing games in the street, riding a bicycle without lights, gambling, obscene language and sleeping rough. If late 20th century standards of policing and sentences had been applied in Edwardian Britain, the prisons would have been virtually empty. Conversely, If Edwardian standards were applied in the 1990s then most of the youth of Britain would be in jail.*

Whatever Britain may have been like in the early 1800s, by the middle of the nineteenth century the character, values and actions of the people were changing markedly. From mid-century onwards this change was to be seen in how peaceful the country was becoming. This peacefulness was not one imposed from above by a tyrannical state; rather, it was the product of an English character which then itself strengthened the forces of self-regulation. The most common state agency encountered by ordinary families was the post office, and the only visible state employee was the policeman. Indeed, for most working people a century ago, the post office was probably what they thought the state was. So how do we account for this quite remarkable transformation?

Three forces have been seminal in Britain having a culture of respect. First, it is impossible to comprehend

*Jose Harris, *Private Lives, Public Spirit: A Social History of Britain, 1870–1914* (Oxford: Oxford University Press, 1993), p. 210.

how British society functioned, particularly over the past 200 years, without appreciating the central importance of Christianity. Within the history of Christianity in Britain, one period of extraordinary growth was marked by what is called the evangelical revival. In this revival the roots of Britain's great journey to respectability are to be found. Evangelical morality, as the historian Noel Annan observed, 'was the single most widespread influence in Victorian England'.* It taught a simple, comprehensive public creed of what was expected of each and every one of us. Its central message was that each would be judged by their actions. Moreover, the judgements, once made, were backed up by a comprehensive set of rewards and punishments. Personal responsibility to oneself, family and neighbours was central to this new cosmos. A new public ideology was established which gave everyone's life a sense of order, structure and purpose, although, of course, no one then thought of it in such terms.

It is easy to mock such ideas and with them the incessant activity such as that shown by Hannah More, in the pre-Victorian age, as she flooded the market with 'improving tracts'. But to do so is to opt out of any attempt to stand in the shoes of our ancestors, to try and understand who and which forces motivated them. Today's Britain is so different

*Noel Annan, *Leslie Stephen: The Godless Victorian* (London: Random House, 1984), p. 146.

from the world I am describing that a journey into the past in a time machine is required if we are not only to meet our Victorian and Edwardian ancestors but also to understand how they viewed the world. Using this time machine, if we could move back a hundred years, we would see that we were not only in a different country but even in a different world.

Victorian society was one governed by the book. Countless numbers of individuals and families lived out their lives in accordance with what they believed the book taught them. The Bible was a practical guide to their lives in a way that Muslims regard the Quran. The literature of late nineteenth-century and Edwardian Britain illustrates what I mean. The village labourers so finely detailed in Flora Thompson's *Lark Rise to Candleford* had a sense of living a religion that can be seen in much of the Muslim world today. The cosmology is almost identical. Their operating framework was to view the world through the eyes of God, an outlook that would now be foreign and incomprehensible to most British people.

Christianity in Victorian society was the great engine shaping the human spirit and character, but the range and depth of adherence were not to be maintained. No sooner did evangelicalism sweep the country than Doubt, with a capital D, began to take hold of a growing part of the public imagination. At the very peak of Victorian Christianity large numbers of the population had already abandoned attending church or chapel — if indeed they had ever done so.

R. H. Tawney, following Matthew Arnold's imagery, compared the loss of a practising Christian adherence in Britain to that of a great ocean receding from the shores of our island. But even as the tide of active adherence turned, it left behind a rich deposit of ethical values that was quickly ploughed by a Labour movement determined to give its creed a very distinctive English DNA. These moral deposits similarly provided the most fertile ground on which to grow and nurture the public ideology of English Idealism which swept in on a new high tide of moral earnestness.

Clichéd though it is, the observation of the former general secretary of the Labour Party, Morgan Phillips, that the Labour movement owes more to Methodism than Marxism nonetheless holds a great truth. How could it be otherwise? The force of the evangelical revival did not somehow miraculously stop at the doorposts of those families who were to become the leaders and foot soldiers of what became known as the Labour movement.

Such a view has not, however, gone uncontested. The senior socialist historian E. P. Thompson wrote that 'the working class did not rise like the sun at an appointed time. It was present at its own making.'* Thompson argues that the working class of the early nineteenth century was the

---

*E. P. Thompson, 'Preface' to *The Making of the English Working Class* (Harmondsworth: Penguin, 1980), p. 8.

product neither of paternalism nor of Methodism but of a high degree of conscious self-effort.

In a glorious attempt to give pride of place to the teams of working people who had been drowned by what he described as the condescension of posterity, Thompson changed how history is written. Against the high politics of statesmen and rulers, Thompson billed the forgotten voices of working people who, between 1780 and 1832, he believed, forged a shared identity and shared interest against their employers to become the English working class. But was a working class in existence to witness its own birth?

Hardly — yet there was a high degree of conscious self-effort in their own making. Gradually, working people realized that if they acted collectively, they had the strength to mitigate the grosser vulgarities and cruelties of early capitalism. They also realized they could change the type of people they were by developing and living out in their everyday lives values that shaped and ennobled their characters. It is within these self-imposed rules, governing their personal lives as well as their friendly societies, co-operatives and trade unions, that we see most clearly the values working people were trying to develop. Here a culture of decency emerged, centred on respect for themselves, for their families, colleagues and neighbours.

Let me cite Thompson on the rules adopted by the membership, and from which the watchwords of the new society emerged. The rulebooks of these organizations,

emphasizing, as they did, 'decency and regularity' (and
we might add 'order'), ring out a clear message that
here were groups of people intent on raising the general
standard of behaviour. Guidelines and sanctions were also
seen as crucial to a successful outcome: behaving badly
to other members – striking another person, being drunk
on a Sunday, taking God's name in vain – would attract
a fine. So would answering back to a steward or speaking
over another member. Betting in the club was outlawed,
and offenders were fined. Anyone drawing sick pay from
a friendly society or a trade union who was found to be
drinking or gaming would similarly be penalized. The
language of friendly societies, mutual aid bodies and trade
unions joined the language of Christian charity to what
Thompson in somewhat curmudgeonly fashion concedes
to be the 'slumbering imagery of "brotherhood" in the
Methodist (and Moravian) tradition'.[*]

The wealth and range of these working-class activities
also gave a particular shape to British society. It was not
so much that Britain became a nation of club members.
That was and remains true. But these clubs, friendly
societies, mutual aid organizations and trade unions began
developing a distinctive character among their members
while simultaneously, and without fanfare, and probably

---

[*]Thompson, *The Making of the English Working Class*, p. 462.

without any conscious design, bringing into existence a public domain that became self-policing.

This public domain is not to be confused with the post-1945 one-dimensional view which equated nationalization with the public domain. The state would be looked to for providing a framework of law to protect the domain's common activities. Still, no one thought it was the state's responsibility to provide the services that operated here. Indeed, there was a healthy scepticism about whose side the state stood on. The doctrine of the public sphere was developed a stage further by an ideology which saw the public domain as fundamental to the development of an active and full citizenship, which was itself a central objective of English Idealism, as well as of other movements.

I referred earlier to the rich deposits of ethical values left behind as the great tide of evangelical Christianity receded from its near-domination of English culture. It was on this fertile ground that a new public ideology took root. Most of those Victorians who became plagued by doubt about the essential Christian truths hoped, nevertheless, that Christian morality would survive without being underpinned by Christian dogma. The reason why this impressive Victorian elite, described by Noel Annan as an intellectual aristocracy, saw their hopes fulfilled for so long a period of time was that Christian values were both taken up by an incipient Labour movement and transformed into a public ideology known as English Idealism.

Herein lies a paradox. Most schools of philosophy are concerned with winning the adherence of other philosophers. (It is an anorak's occupation par excellence.) But it was not so with English Idealism. It provided a secular home for those who found it impossible fully to subscribe to Christian beliefs, but who wished to see the Christian ethic continue. They saw their task as putting old wine into new bottles and, despite the New Testament warnings on the danger, they achieved a demonstrable success. English Idealism had a distinct political goal: to provide a framework of ideas within which the minds of those set on rising to positions of power in the British Empire would be trained.

Some observers, such as the historian R. G. Collingwood, argue that English Idealism was at its most influential between 1880 and 1910. Others, such as Jose Harris, have suggested that its importance spread beyond the First World War and swept up to the 1945 Labour government of Clement Attlee. The one set of lectures that Attlee later recalled as having influenced his ideas were those delivered at Oxford in his undergraduate days by Ernest Barker, one of the most distinguished members of the second generation of English Idealists.

I would argue that the influence of English Idealism, though in decline, can be seen right up to the Tony Blair administration, providing, as it did, a framework within which Blair thought about politics.

Despite a tortuous Germanic shell, the kernel of English Idealism was easily expressed and had a wide appeal to men and women in raising their children and running local civic societies. A great motor force in life was the belief that each of us should achieve our best self and that society should be so organized that this goal is an effective option for every member of the community. It was this belief which not only bound individuals and families together but also formed the basis of public ideology which ran alongside, and then largely superseded, Christianity.

English Idealism had two additional attractions that helped secure its commanding position as a public ideology. While today what little talk there is of citizenship is mainly confined to discussions about voting – or rather, lack of it – the citizenship underpinning English Idealism was much more generous and expansive. At its centre was the ideal of a virtuous character. In this respect, it aimed to make universal the kind of citizenship that had been the preserve of a few in Ancient Greek democracy.

English Idealism's success induced further success. A public ideology, governing so much of public conduct, gave what would now appear to be an unimaginable degree of confidence to those whose role was to initiate the young into the wider community. Those ever so important foot soldiers of any society, the clergy, teachers, police, factory and health inspectors, doctors, voluntary workers and a growing host of other officials, went about their task with assurance. While they attended directly to the issues that gave rise to their position – teaching or policing, for example – they knew their work fitted into a larger picture.

They were committed to this wider goal of improving the type of character they and their charges possessed. They also knew that, if push came to shove, they would be unquestionably backed by society's most influential people. Here are important lessons for us to bear in mind when we come to consider what options are open to us today.

11

The Balkanization of This Peaceable Kingdom

How, then, do we account for what I call the Balkanization of this peaceable kingdom? The most obvious cause for our present discontent is that the writ of the three chief forces that shaped the British character no longer runs as it once did. Christianity, Labour's mutual commonwealth and the public ideology of English Idealism are all but a shadow of their former selves. However, English Idealism still has a strong pull on our senses. But let me emphasize again that I am in no way making a plea that our political efforts should go into trying to restore this old order. I do not believe for one moment that this option is open to us. But when we come to thinking about the practical measures we might take, it is always important to understand that each of these influences was not a marginal afterthought for the shaping of character; they were all seminal. Nor was their influence felt immediately. On the contrary, there was a cumulative effect over time. Similar influential and favourable forces are required now if a counter-push against the growth of present-day nihilism is to be successful.

Aside from our neglectfulness and failure to renew this aspect of our cultural–political heritage, our peaceful kingdom is being undermined by proactive forces and we need to turn our attention to them. Here I see a number of agents working in the same destructive direction. Top of the list has been the meltdown of semi-skilled jobs in manufacturing, of administrative and middle management jobs in services through digitization. Following hard on its heels, but inseparably linked to it, has been the sharp increase in the number of parents who fail to teach their children the common decencies. Third, the 1944 Butler Education Act creamed off most of the able-bodied working-class children and made them socially, and often geographically, mobile. In so doing, it left those children's neighbours bereft of their leadership and organizing skills. Fourth, a growing and now dominant culture has been established where the individual more often than not reigns supreme over any collective or public ethos. No single one of these causes alone is responsible for the trends so apparent in British society. However, the cumulative impact of all of them – and of others – is little short of devastating.

Since I first entered the House of Commons, the structure of the British economy changed from one of extraction (mining), heavy industry (steel, shipbuilding) and manufacturing (cars) to one of services. As Member of Parliament for Birkenhead I lived through this painful period, representing the unemployed.

The Mersey Docks and Harbour Board employed in the earlier post-war period something like 16,000 dockers. These men – no women were employed in this trade – handled an import and export trade from and into the Liverpool and Birkenhead docks which was then measured around 26 million tons per annum. Then the number of dockers was reduced to 460, yet they were responsible for handling 32 million tons or so of goods coming into and leaving the port. Moreover, the loss of well over 15,000 semi-skilled jobs that paid decent family wages played a part in the rise of more than one generation that had no serious job opportunities – the financial basis for long-term partnership, marriage and the raising of children.

The loss of the dock's jobs, and of those skilled jobs lost in the Cammell Laird shipyard, quickly wiped out the job opportunities of a very significant part of the male workforce in the town. While there has been an increase in male jobs in Britain since 1951 of nearly 20 per cent, Birkenhead saw a fall of 35 per cent. But this total, as so often with a global figure, disguises a polarization of opportunities. The constituency has witnessed over the same time a significant increase in people who are self-employed, have employee status or are following professional careers. This is in stark contrast to the almost 60 per cent drop in the numbers of less skilled jobs. These data are similar to those for other poorer areas, and they help to account for a growth in estranged young unskilled workers who populate the poorest areas in the country and whose badge of citizenship is often expressed in yobbish behaviour.

More recently, there has been a significant growth in jobs outside the constituency, particularly on the North Welsh coast. But the scale of the semi-skilled job losses has impacted behaviour in a number of ways. Both the docks and the shipyard were dangerous places in which to work, even if everybody maintained a proper sense of discipline. This degree of order established at work rippled over into the town, and the loss of this discipline, and the pride that went with it, have had an impact on the level of order in the wider community. From the earliest time of industrialization, order in large industrial complexes was maintained by employers and trade unions alike. Today, fewer people work in similarly large establishments in Birkenhead or elsewhere. Most now work in smaller units which do not share this collective sense.

This changing employment status, and particularly the massive haemorrhage of semi-skilled jobs, have had a significant impact on the marriage prospects of many males. It seems strange even to say this, but it is true nevertheless. A key function historically of adult males has been to bring home a family wage. Being a financial provider was one of the most widely understood functions of a husband and father, and it was a role that provided status, influence and dignity. The local ecology of family formation has been fundamentally altered by the meltdown of traditional well-paid male jobs.

The flip side of this trend has been the rise of single-parent families. While there are notable exceptions to any rule, young boys find it more difficult to negotiate successfully their teenage years if they do not have a male model providing an ordered existence as they become of age. It is a truism to say that raising children is a task that can sometimes defeat the best of two parents, let alone just one.

We need to add to this the losing of parental skills more generally among the population. It is no coincidence that Britain becoming a peaceable kingdom was linked to a period of stable and generally confident families. However, these confident families did not emerge from a vacuum. But it is within families that the ethical building blocks of any community are forged for good or ill. A measure of successful families is the growth in the respect each member holds for the others, and this is where one's own sense of respect takes root.

It is within the family, too, that we develop the three cardinal virtues that underpin our respect for others: a degree of *politeness*, which makes one respectful of the needs of others; a *considerateness*, whereby the needs of other members of the family as well as neighbours bear down on an individual's behaviour; and lastly, a degree of *thoughtfulness*, the development of which helps us to determine what another person's needs and feelings are.

The Butler education reforms of 1944 had a perverse impact on local neighbourhoods and weakened still further an already battered family structure. Whatever the conventional wisdom about this great reform, the Act ensured that able, working-class boys and girls were 'creamed off' and pointed towards jobs that would in all too many instances take them away from their local communities.

While this reform was beneficial to the individuals concerned, and society generally, it had a major impact in that it robbed local communities of many of its natural leaders. Individuals whose strength of character placed them into leadership roles, and who were natural living role models of decent behaviour, have long since quit their humble backgrounds for a life elsewhere. Trade unions and local authorities have similarly been weakened by the loss of these high-achieving individuals, while mutual aid organizations of any size have almost disappeared.

All of the factors I have just discussed have led to a process of disruption of the peaceable kingdom. The prophesying witches in Macbeth chanted, 'Hubble, bubble, toil and trouble.' In today's equivalent of the witches' cauldron of skilled and semi-skilled job losses and broken families, this has stirred the inexorable rise of an individualistic culture. This culture operates on two levels. The first is that it is blind to the rules of engagement that once policed the public domain we all enter as we close our front doors. Rules regulating the self-respect of people living in close proximity to each other, and which were crafted out of necessity, are now bulldozed by the defiant cry of 'Why?'

And the plain truth is that it is impossible for a society to survive whose basic rules of engagement are subjected to this destructive question. There simply is not the time or the energy constantly to go back to first principles and explain the purpose of a particular rule. So the question 'Why?' conquers ever more territory, reducing it to little more than anarchy. This individualism has been added and speeded up by a social media where individuals are given free rein over whatever instincts they have, without any personal responsibility for what they say.

On a second level, a culture glorifying the here and now strips away any sense of being responsible for one's own actions. This culture change has been so profound that it is difficult to see how that world we have now lost is joined to the world in which we now inhabit. Some of the best examples of an ethic of non-responsibility come from Theodore Dalrymple, whose work as a hospital and prison psychiatrist gave him an insight into this way of life that is little short of terrifying. The 'beer went mad ... the knife went in' are actions which allegedly control the individual rather than the other way round.

There is one last factor which must be taken into account when trying to explain the Balkanization of peaceful Britain. It is the carelessness, taken to the point of irresponsibility, with which we have not attended to reinvesting in the social capital that underpinned our peaceable kingdom. The country has sleepwalked away from an acknowledgement that the kind of citizenship we had inherited is one which has to be constantly worked out, modified and, above all, renewed.

The rich concept of citizenship that we inherited did not come down from Mount Sinai already engraved on tablets of stone and able to weather the blast of changing social norms. Rather, our ancestors knew that the kind of citizens we are is almost totally dependent on the forces that shape our collective character. And, as I have argued here, our inheritance on this score was the product of the ethic built up by Christian morality, the Labour movement reflecting this ethic in its own institutions, and the hugely powerful set of social rules which English Idealism laid down for the whole country. While only a mere skeleton is left of these three forces, it was widely assumed that somehow the type of character that these forces produced would continue. No effort, until recently, has been put into developing a new public ideology which could compensate for those we have lost. Once the 1945 nationalizing programme had been enacted, Clement Attlee decreed that the next great task of the Labour movement was to develop armies of socialist characters to run the new institutions. The consequences of the failure to do this were slow to appear, and most of us, including myself at first, were reluctant to accept that the peaceable world that we had once inhabited was being destroyed before our very eyes. Then the pace of disintegration suddenly and rapidly changed.

For all of these reasons and more – a drink and drugs culture and a social media which gives a certain degree of anonymity to bullying and uncivilized behaviour – the culture of respect is now under sustained and heavy bombardment. While it is now the number one issue so far as my former constituents are concerned, it was far from being so when I was first elected MP for Birkenhead. I would receive during the earlier part of this stewardship occasional reports of loutish and even thuggish behaviour. But these citings were at first very irregular. Even when such examples of the breakdown of civility were reported to me on a more regular basis I continued to compartmentalize them as appalling actions. They were definitely exceptions.

I realized over time that these yobbish events were becoming pivotal to a growing number of my constituents. The agenda had suddenly changed, and my constituents helped me to define it. The politics of class, in which I had learned what political skills I had, was fast being replaced by the politics of behaviour. British politics was in uncharted territory, with no ethical compass to give direction. There were no off-the-shelf solutions that practising politicians could simply hand to their constituents. Politics had to be remade to match the new circumstances.

The task was doubly challenging. Reform is invariably a difficult and often hazardous process. But some reforms are easier to achieve than others. Modernizing the National Health Service might be complex and demanding, but at least the service is in existence. Moreover, because the government has been running the service for nearly 75 years, it brings to the task of reform a great deal of technical and practical knowledge of what might and might not work. It also has some feel for the most likely indirect consequences of any particular reform.

Not so with the politics of respect. Here governments have had very little record until recently of involvement. Britain's long march to respectability, as we have seen, was one that originated with and was organized by the people, without government interference. Indeed, government action in the moulding of behaviour would not only have been thought of as dangerous but would also have been an unacceptable intrusion into those areas where no government should tread.

Similarly, because politics are in new territory, mistakes and misjudgements are more likely to be made. Politicians will have to acquire new skills (not something they relish) – to create new policies but also a willingness to admit quickly to what is working and, more importantly, what is not. In forging this new agenda it is important to realize that the outcome is of greatest importance to what were once Labour's core voters.

I LOSE
BIRKENHEAD

12

I'm Out: Momentum Remains

For significant parts of my political life, Labour had been unelectable. A main reason for this had been the influence of Trotskyism and the hard left. My activities against the Trotskyites became part of the Labour Party's struggle to regain the trust of the electorate. Here I recall my last and most significant fights with the hard left, which ended my House of Commons career.

I nominated Jeremy Corbyn as a candidate in the leadership contest to succeed Ed Miliband back in 2015. Immediately the questioning was how could I possibly have done such a thing, given that Jeremy Corbyn was and always had been part of the hard left group. What does the defence case for my action look like? And would I have nominated Corbyn if I believed there was any possibility of him winning?

The second question can be dealt with immediately. Had I thought for the shortest second available to man- and womankind that Jeremy Corbyn would win the Labour leadership contest, I would never have nominated him. I did not believe he could win, and this judgement was shared by those on the hard left who thought their chances of success were nil. In a broadcast interview John McDonnell, who was a senior Corbynite, told his audience that when the hard left group met in one of the Commons committee rooms to decide upon a candidate, there were no volunteers. None of the main characters could see the pathway to a successful leadership challenge. John reminded the meeting that he had fought the leadership contest once already and that he had done his duty. Moreover, he had had a heart attack. So the questioning went on. Diane Abbott likewise refused the offer of being the hard left candidate as she had already contested the leadership once and, like the other candidates hardened by the battle, couldn't see the value of such a pointless exercise again. And so the gnashing of teeth went on in an atmosphere where the group had a duty to put forward a candidate, but there was no one at the meeting with a stomach for a fight they all thought they would lose. At some point the questioning was directed at Corbyn. He hadn't done his duty as a candidate and so, finally, the hard left had a name to put forward and around whom they would conduct a leadership campaign.

Jeremy had served on the Health and Social Services Health committee I chaired during the 1992–7 Parliament, when, as the rules decreed, the Tories had a majority on the committee to reflect their overall majority in the House of Commons. Yet, although we published as many reports as any other committee, and although all the reports were ones I wished to see published as a means of radicalizing the welfare state debate, every report was recommended unanimously by the committee to the House of Commons. Jeremy signed up.

Labour MPs have the role of nominating candidates they would wish to see participate in the leadership contest and, for the vast majority of them, win that contest. Jeremy, who was now a candidate, talked to me for the first time ever, including all the committee sessions, when he came up to thank me for nominating him. I was so surprised at being spoken these five words by him that my answer simply jumped out. 'I won't be voting for you.' 'I never expected that you would' came the equally quick reply.

So why the nomination?

While I have never thought of myself as having any affinity with the hard left, what they defined as their socialist views have a place in the Labour Party, providing they subscribe to a form of party democracy that the electorate recognize as a distinct British variant of democracy. I had no wish to see the hard left's ideas dominate. However, I did and still do believe that it is crucial for different sectors of the party to be able to contribute to its local and national debate, since such debate is where the nuance of democracy needs to be practised. Such views need to be audible and taken into account but not dominating. I wished the Corbynite views to play a part in the leadership contest, to help influence the outcome but not to dominate the outcome. Once Corbyn was in power, the hard left's total domination of the debate was served up as a form of party democracy.

Here I need to go back a little to recall the attempts I had made (along with others, of course) to see the Labour Party become more democratic and, by this route, to see the electorate's trust in the party being significantly increased.

I was concerned even in 1979 about how much longer Labour would be able to remain one of the two main political parties. A new deal was needed, with the role of individual members extended. The aim was to re-create a party where many more individuals would join because they saw this role as the next step of developing a stronger political culture.

Here was a form of party democracy centred on the proposed wider reform of 'one person, one vote'. In the 'one person, one vote' campaign I was joined by people like the economist Paul Ormerod, the MP Malcolm Wicks (now sadly deceased) and Peter Mandelson. My aim was for this idea to be the new defining factor in Labour's modernization. I aimed for this to be a counter-force to the unbelievably terrible drubbing the party received in the 1983 election at the hands of Mrs Thatcher. In 1980 I had given a note of the idea to Mike Thomas, who was to be the organizational genius behind the SDP. David Owen made the idea of enacting 'one person, one vote' the criterion then for remaining within the Labour Party. The then Labour hierarchy resisted the idea, and we all know what happened.

The campaign of which I was a part saw 'one person, one vote' become a defining operational principle of Labour Party democracy. 'One person, one vote' would decide major policy decisions, and 'one person, one vote' would be the mechanism by which candidates for Parliament, and to other bodies, were chosen. In party leadership contests MPs would have the duty to nominate a candidate for the party leadership, and the party activists would vote from the MPs' list of names that had enough nominations. To decide the contest 'one person, one vote' would also determine who were candidates for Parliament and local authorities. In introducing this reform it was assumed that the age-old rules aimed at protecting the Labour Party from extremist infiltration would continue to operate: i.e., party membership would be critically controlled to prevent extremist infiltration. In the 2015 leadership contest the defences against extremist groups burrowing their way into the Labour Party were abolished. Normally, once a contest was declared, no one was allowed to join the party.

Labour, under Ed Miliband's leadership, made a fatal error that resulted in Corbyn being elected. This time Ed Miliband used the contest to introduce a very cheap party membership which would give new members the right to help elect the next party leader. Anybody could join, and some Tories openly joined the Labour Party and said that they would be voting for Jeremy Corbyn as this would be of most advantage to them. Not only did a few Tories join, but so did massive numbers of other people too, many of them with Trotskyite sympathies. The hard left saw the unique opportunity this party reform offered them and acted ruthlessly. Labour under Ed Miliband lowered the party's protective shield against those groups which historically had tried to destroy the Labour Party. Many of them piled into the Labour Party to vote for Corbyn. Corbyn won.

The National Labour Party had a huge lead-in time to my resignation of the Labour whip. Seven months before my curt dismissal I had given a party one Saturday lunchtime for friends and supporters in Birkenhead after many of us had completed our Saturday morning campaigning session. About 60 people came. It was early days, I explained, but every example of bullying, and the accompanying uncouth behaviour to which some party members were being subjected to an ever-growing extent, had been submitted to the regional and national party for disciplinary action. Every one of these attempts to restore the operation of civilized values had been knocked back by the Labour Party bureaucracy, generally by ignoring each detailed complaint and submission. Most submissions gained no response at all. Others were simply acknowledged. To this group of friends I committed myself to resign the whip if I didn't get justice, and particularly for Walter Smith.

Walter was chair of the Birkenhead Labour Party in that January of 1979 when the local party chose me as the Labour candidate for Birkenhead to replace the retiring distinguished MP, Edmund Dell. Walter came from a strongly committed nonconformist family and remained a nonconformist all his life. His father, a craft trade union leader, had in the 1920s been chair of his trade union's annual conference. It is difficult to imagine anyone having a purer nature than Walter.

The local Labour Party met together on the fourth Friday of every month. At the October 2017 meeting one of the leading Momentum supporters, who was also a councillor, tried to move a motion against me for alleged attempts to undermine the National Minimum Wage policy. Here was an example of the Trotskyite and Momentum group tactics, ever anxious to peddle the worst, however untrue, in their attempts to undermine the credibility of an elected Labour MP who would not bend to their agenda.

This councillor had already tried to get Wirral Council to condemn me on the score of attacking the minimum wage. At the council gathering she had failed miserably. Now at the Labour Party meeting she again attacked what she said was my stance on the minimum wage. Once she had completed her attack, I welcomed the chance to reject the absurdity of it. Back in 1974 I'd established the Low Pay Unit with the immediate task of ensuring that wages councils (bodies charged to establish minimum wages for certain industrial groups of low-paid workers) should meet regularly to set a new minimum wage. Some of these councils had not met for well over a decade. Running alongside our campaign on wages councils, we lobbied to gain a legally backed wage for all workers as part of a joint campaign with the National Union of Public employees (Nupe) for a National Minimum Wage (details of this campaign are in Chapter 7).

Walter joined in the debate and told the meeting that the attack had failed to get any support in the council. After the meeting, as we were leaving, Walter went over to his colleague, and there the matter rested, or so I thought. While Walter was speaking to his fellow councillor, I was in the same hall talking to people.

Following this meeting, allegations were made to the police alleging that Walter had physically assaulted the other councillor. Walter was questioned under caution. The caution had the most dramatic impact on him. He told one of his fellow councillors that he was so ashamed of such a wicked allegation that was being made against him. He felt unclean. Betty, his wife, who had been his sweetheart since they were both 15-year-olds, had died earlier that year. She, and Walter's parents, would be looking down from heaven to witness the police questioning him under caution. Two weeks later Walter, who was still a regular runner with his local running club, even though he was aged 82, died of a massive heart attack while working at his tailoring business.

Walter Smith was kind and full of goodness, never holding a grudge against anyone, as far as I could judge. In some instances, I thought he was too tolerant of the intolerance around us. The idea that this man could suffer a heart attack after a lifetime of service in the Labour movement without the National Labour Party lifting a finger to enquire as to the circumstances surrounding his death appalled me. A characteristic of totalitarianism has always been a total disregard for individual life. A pattern of events was beginning to emerge clearly that showed how the Corbyn Labour Party would behave if it ever formed a government.

I pledged to members and friends at that Saturday lunch that, if I failed to get the National Labour Party to adjudicate in what I regarded as trumped-up charges against Walter, I would resign the whip. Time and time again I requested specific action about Walter's case from the national party, as did some other party members. No action at all was forthcoming. We never received a formal reply to any of these requests. Our adroit Chief Whip in the Commons sought action. Again, no meaningful action was forthcoming.

At this time Jeremy Corbyn was cultivating a national tolerance of the thuggery that we were experiencing locally from Momentum activists. The National Labour Party was also harbouring anti-Semites. All too many of Jeremy's past associations were with groupings who believed it was legitimate to use violence to achieve their political ends, including many such organizations committed to wiping Israel off the face of the map. I resigned the whip on 30 August 2018 over Jeremy's failure to counter anti-Semitism, and over all the examples other members and I had submitted to the party detailing the intolerance against many local members by Momentum over many years, on which the national Party showed not the slightest intention of taking any action. Those who were bullied, and those who submitted complaints, were from different parts of the party who did not owe their allegiance to Momentum.

I am, by nature, ever looking forward to new events and new reforms. But the then current deep calamity and wretchedness in the Labour Party had bought me up sharp. The horror of Militant activists in the early 1980s had fallen away into a deep part of my memory. Then, all of a sudden, those memories were snatched out of that far recess of my mind and replayed, this time with a Militant and Momentum line-up. Those malevolent events of lying, cheating, bullying and the like, which were the stuff of Militant politics, were now centre-stage and appealing to a wider membership that carried this hateful DNA.

The counting of the votes in my first election in 1979 had hardly been completed when I was warned by the full-time paid Militant organizer in Birkenhead that, if I didn't take their line, I would be deselected before the next election. A huge power struggle erupted between local Labour Party loyalists and the Militant faction, with Michael Foot, then the leader of the Parliamentary Labour Party, saying that if Birkenhead was lost, so would be the Labour Party.

What was the point of being an MP if I could only serve Birkenhead on their terms, rather than trying to interpret for myself what I believed to be best for Birkenhead? Once it became clear that I was not prepared to accept their diktat, party meetings became chaotic. Militant member after Militant member got up to tell the most shocking lies about me. Every new lie left me aghast. What sort of machine did they have to think up such a campaign?

I would regularly wake up during the night, my heart thumping, as the next meeting with Militant approached. One morning, at the height of these incidents, I had finished showering and was shaving when I found myself thinking about my need to face the Trots at our monthly Labour Party meeting. Such was the fear that I vomited. I looked into the mirror at my pathetic face, with sick all over my shaving cream. I said to myself that I could think of any number of excuses that would appear plausible for not appearing at that night's meeting. But if I so acted, I knew I would not simply be running away from a single meeting, but would be running away from such conflicts for the rest of my life. To the meeting I went.

Three decades later, Momentum had joined forces with those from Militant who were still knocking around and had been welcomed back into the party by the leadership.

On one occasion, when speaking with Nick Brown, 'our' then Chief Whip, about my failure to get the national party to act against the bullying and intolerance that were Momentum's weapon to gain control of the Birkenhead Labour Party, he had asked me not to take any action about resigning the whip until I had spoken to him first. I then still thought of myself as Labour – hence the quotation marks around 'our'. On 30 August 2018 I took my resignation letter over to the opposition Chief Whip's office in the House of Commons. Nick was busy in his Newcastle constituency. I therefore phoned to say that I had asked for my resignation letter to be scanned and sent to him. The letter had already been released to the media.

'Why hadn't I spoken to him first?' was his immediate response. Nick had been kind to me on a number of occasions since our membership of the House overlapped. I replied that I hadn't done so because he might have persuaded me not to resign and I knew that would be the wrong course of action. I told him, in order to strengthen my resolve, that there was no going back, that I had released the letter to the media. The conversation moved quickly. To which MPs had I spoken, Nick immediately inquired. 'None,' I replied. 'You are the first.' 'You are not, then, part of a wider campaign against Jeremy's leadership, or part of the Remain group of MPs seeking to gain a second referendum?' 'No,' I replied, laughing, 'you bet I'm not.' 'I couldn't see you as part of that group' was Nick's reply.

Nick had been finishing his constituency work that day but was coming back to London the following morning. Could we talk then? Yes, I replied. While Nick had meetings all day, he told me that he would clear his room and talk to me any time my diary allowed.

Only later did I realize the importance of Nick's questioning: he had clearly got wind of a breakaway group of eight Labour MPs that six months later left the

Parliamentary Labour Party to form Change UK. A day later I went over to his Commons office, crossing from mine in Portcullis House, the newish office block for MPs built on the other side of the road from the House of Commons. Nick greeted me by saying we should go through the formal side of my resignation.

I had two weeks to reconsider and withdraw my resignation. If I didn't, I would cease to be a Labour Party member. I gasped. I never thought for one moment I would lose my party membership. I never viewed resigning the whip as a capital offence. Nor had anyone suggested that it was. At the party back in January I had assured the assembled group of Labour Party friends that, while I intended to resign the whip in Parliament should I fail to get an inquiry for Walter, I emphasized that I would be remaining a Labour Party member, as I had been for very nearly 60 years.

Nick passed me a single sheet of A4 paper and there stood a couple of sentences reproduced from Labour's rule book. The rule that would end my party membership read: 'All Labour MPs shall be members of the Parliamentary Labour Party (PLP) and play their part in its work.' I still very much saw myself as a Labour MP in every aspect of my work, while I continued to fight for justice against the bullying and thuggery in the Birkenhead Labour Party.

'This doesn't apply to me, Nick,' I responded, as I sat in his office, he in a chair by his desk and I on one of his two sofas in his office. I shall legally contest this ruling's applicability to me, I kept muttering. In my letter of resignation I expressed that, should the Labour Party nationally take firm action to deal with the intolerance that was engulfing the Birkenhead Labour Party, I would wish to seek the Labour whip.

On to other business. Labour MPs pay 2 per cent of their salary towards covering the staff costs of a service to MPs. Would I be prevented from paying this sum, I asked? No, but the contribution couldn't be enforced upon me as with other members of the PLP. Any further contributions I made would be viewed as a donation.

Nick reminded me that my set of office rooms was allocated to the Labour Party and I could be turfed out. For the first time in my 40-year life in Parliament I had near-perfect offices. Nick had talked with his fellow whips. On the basis that I was a senior member of Parliament, a Privy Councillor and Chair of a Select Committee, Nick had said that I would remain in my offices. A huge sense of relief came over me.

Nick handed me the statement of the whip for the following week that had gone to Labour MPs, telling us (them) when we would be required to vote when the House returned. 'Having the whip didn't make much impression on your behaviour when you were a member of the PLP. Might I ask you to try and improve your voting record in supporting the whip from now on,' Nick quipped. I laughed out loud. Nick was referring to my votes on Brexit, which had been consistent with the party's manifesto commitment to implement the Brexit decision and with how, in fact, Birkenhead had voted: in line with the whole country, with a tally of 52 per cent to leave and 48 per cent to stay.

The votes for Brexit were not votes for Tory legislation, as Momentum kept maintaining. Both parties during the referendum campaign had promised to bring forward the necessary legislation to implement the referendum result if it was for leaving. Labour was committed to bringing forward a Withdrawal Agreement upon which the House of Commons would be required to vote, had it won the election. The line was pushed by the extreme left that Labour MPs were being called upon to vote for Tory legislation, and gained adherence in some unexpected places, including with the then Prime Minister herself. On one vote Theresa May came up to me and thanked me for being in her lobby. 'Oh no, Prime Minister,' I replied, 'you're in my lobby.' A second passed before she gave one of her great bursts of laughter. I had always been, on balance, a 'Leaver' ever since the 1975 referendum. It was Mrs May, the Remainer, who was voting in my lobby.

More importantly, the idea that Brexit legislation was a Tory measure was to play a crucial part in Momentum's door-to-door campaigning in the election: I was a Tory stooge, and a vote for me was a vote against ever having a Labour government. It was as successful in Birkenhead as it was misplaced in those 'red wall' Labour seats that fell to the Tories.

Knowing that I would be expected within two weeks to make a decision on whether I stood firm on resigning the whip, I'd commented to the media that I hoped that I would have the best legal minds to fight the party's decision to expel me, and to safeguard my nearly 60 years' party membership. I was thinking here of Nick Warren. Nick and his family had come to Birkenhead shortly after I was elected as an MP. He established a welfare rights body to help the Birkenhead MP, and all the local councillors, whatever their political affiliations, so as to defend the interests of their poorer constituents.

He was brilliant in his service to constituents and this service was unique in the whole country. An endless, endless number of constituents gained redress from injustice through Nick's work and, as part of this, Nick had taken class actions to the Divisional Court. Class actions were very much in favour in the USA at the time as I joined CPAG in 1969. Three of Mrs Thatcher's welfare bills had been introduced to overthrow Nick's class action successes.

It was Nick I turned to first to ask advice on how I should respond to being expelled from the Labour Party. These comments in the media that I wanted to have the best legal advice available brought forth a witty email from Mishcon de Reya. (This was the firm that had negotiated Princess Diana's divorce and, more recently, Margaret Hodge's right to pin down Jeremy Corbyn's association with anti-Semitism.) Mishcon de Reya had assumed I was referring to them when wishing to have the best legal representation going into battle on my behalf. James Lisbon and Harry Eccles-Williams at Mishcon de Reya proved to be worth their weight in gold. Nick, Andrew Forsey, who headed my parliamentary office, and Clive Sheldon, the QC commissioned by Mishcon de Reya to give an opinion, all agreed that the Labour Party bureaucrats had no grounds for expelling me.

When I met Nick Brown on that fateful day after my resignation, I was told I would have two weeks to withdraw my resignation of the Labour whip and thereby keep my party membership. There was no two-week delay. I had, of course, no intention of withdrawing my resignation of the whip, but the Madame Defarge sitting under the Labour Party guillotine wrote for once within days with chilling efficiency. A letter headed with my Labour Party membership number of 60 years told me that I was out of the party.

This letter of execution also told me that, now I was no longer a Labour Party member, my complaints of the thuggish behaviour by some Momentum members in Wirral were no longer being considered. I stress this action as it suggests that Labour Party bureaucrats believe either that they are above the law or that no law applies to them. The Labour Party is a corporate body, and anyone, member or not, has a right to have complaints about the conduct of members of corporate bodies considered fully, while attempting to seek redress.

Why did I make all this fuss about my membership of the Labour Party once I had resigned from the party whip? Why did I involve myself in protracted warfare with Jeremy Corbyn and his bureaucracy to overturn their arbitrary decision to expel me?

The answer goes back to that journey I had been making as a sixth-former going to school. I was then seeking a political vehicle that I believed would offer the greatest opportunity to achieve the blend of social and economic justice that I was beginning to make my own. Labour, I decided, of all political parties, was offering me that chance to work for the greater good. I was quite clear then that it wasn't the Labour Party organization to which I was giving my loyalty. It was with the party's ideas, vision and direction of political travel that I wished to join forces. Ironically, the view of my commitment to this extraordinary organization changed, but only as an MP, and only after I began to inquire into the basis of so many Birkenhead's Labour Party members' loyalty to the Labour Party machine.

As I learned more about their virtuous living, and how the Labour Party membership for them was a means for extending their virtuous lives, my attitude to the Labour Party as a corporate body changed. The more I learned from local members, the less I regarded the Labour Party simply as a political vehicle to achieve set goals. Instead, I began to see it more as a society trying to live out a set of political ideas that were widely supported by the membership.

I was 37 years of age when I so proudly became the MP for Birkenhead, a real town with a real history, and a real sense of place and identity. Practically the whole of the Birkenhead Labour Party at that time was then older than I, many of them much older. I set about asking those with the longest membership why they had joined the Labour Party. All had grown old in the struggle for the New Jerusalem. They knew that they would not now reach that goal, but they had, during their life's struggle, passed important landmarks on the way to that end. From that political struggle they expected to gain no personal honour. It was this collective good that they ever wished to see expanded.

One married couple characterized the findings I gained from talking with these local Labour Party stewards, and their family have allowed me to use their real names: Fred and Winnie Johnson. Members who had joined the Labour Party fell into two groups. First, there were those who had been members before the Attlee government; second, there were those who joined as a result of that government's legislative programme to build the New Jerusalem. Fred and Winnie perfectly illustrated these two groups of Labour Party members I interviewed soon after 1979.

Fred had joined the Labour Party before the 1945 Attlee government. I see his smiling face now for it was the face that always greeted me. His face was creased beautifully in smiles. Every conversation began with the same laughing refrain. 'How's the fish and chips today?' Fred was referring to my constant appearance in the local newspapers, whose secondary role was then used for wrapping up this then relatively cheap wonderful food. Fred had joined the party on class terms. He was very clear. Inequality was structural. Only the Labour Party in government could begin to redress those huge grievances suffered by the working class as a whole.

Winnie always had a sense of purposefulness about her, right up to and including the last two times I saw her in a care home. Unlike Fred, Winnie had not joined the Labour Party until Nye Bevan's great reforming NHS Act had begun to take effect. She explained quietly that, before the war, whenever she had a very sick child, she had to cross the local doctor's palm with half a crown before she and her ill child were granted access. Half a crown then was a significant amount of money. She didn't always have half a crown. When she could produce one, it was often at the cost of there being less food for the whole family – which meant primarily her, of course, though Winnie never said so.

As she made these remarks, Winnie held her gaze deep and looked straight into my eyes. It remains one of the most penetrating gazes I've ever encountered. Winnie then said, with the muscles in her face taut, that Labour's NHS had saved her, and every working family, from the most awful and dreadful horror of not always being able to gain help for a sick child. Before the NHS, money was in too many instances a real barrier to accessing medical help. Winnie had made a lifetime's commitment in loyalty to the Labour Party on the basis of the establishment of the NHS alone.

As time went on, and as I attended the funerals of this band of colleagues, my commitment to the party, which they had helped shape with such love and commitment, and the reasons for that commitment, took an ever stronger hold on me. But now I was out of the party. I would fight the next election, and the hard left would appoint the Labour candidate.

I stood as Birkenhead Social Justice candidate but, despite a small bank of loyal supporters headed by the then local councillor Moira McLaughlin and, of course, Andrew Forsey, we were overwhelmed. The hard left bussed in people to work their campaign. One evening, as our small party went into a local pub to eat, I found on the menu a note from the group that was just leaving. It greeted me by saying 'Up from Wokingham to get you.' And so they did.

The result declared that I had over 7,000 votes but this was overwhelmed by the total for the official Labour candidate. I was out and Momentum and the hard left were in.

LOOKING
FORWARD

13

The Dominance of Human Nature in My Political Views

I t is difficult to underestimate the role that human nature plays in all my political ideas. The role of human nature is the DNA running through all the public statements I have made on the political programmes I've tried to advance. Mankind is a fallen creature but, as Christianity teaches, we are born to be redeemed.

While this view of human nature determined the shape of the welfare reforms I proposed, it also shaped all my other major proposals, such as the sale of council houses. It placed limits also on the role that altruism can play in practical politics. Altruism alone is not a powerful, reliable or stable enough base to advance any successful long-term politics, including provision for the poor. Throughout my career I had attempted to promote self-interested altruism.

By this I meant that while, in some extraordinary circumstances, and for a shortish period of time, mankind can express political emotions that are totally altruistic, this form of altruism is not a viable base for longer-term politics. Indeed, the major divide between myself and the Labour Party was that Labour's hierarchy peddled a view centring on pure altruism. To suggest the need to counter fraud schemes in welfare was anathema for them. I continuously argued that this was not a viable basis for long-term politics and that the very best we could do was to appeal to a sense of self-interested altruism.

Here the reader can see why I spent so much of my political life promoting a National Insurance basis for welfare rather than depending on an expanding means-tested state. The reverse of it has sadly happened.

No one doubts on either the left or the right of British Politics that the role of the state is fundamental to achieving a humane society.

The National Insurance system continues to exist, beyond the expectations of experts like Nick Timmins, the former *Financial Times* social policy editor. But the main growth in welfare over recent years has been the means-tested Universal Credit. I advocated a National Insurance form of welfare with a declining means-tested safety net, under a system in which people pay in from their incomes and get supported when they need it. The opposite has occurred, and so Iain Duncan Smith's vision of a means-tested Universal Credit has prevailed. We can survive with Universal Credit at least for the medium term, but I do not believe it is sustainable in the longer term.

Why do I write 'for the medium term'? First, I believe that a means-tested welfare has an instability built into it.

Means tests discourage honesty: once you declare your increases in income you will see a reduction in your benefit. So, while a growing means-tested welfare state might prevail for the present, it will be defeated in the longer term because of how human nature operates. It rewards people for dishonesty rather than the opposite.

All welfare, but particularly that which is means-tested, is open to fraud, or so a Christian view of human nature would teach us. Throughout my political life I have been dubbed right-wing, or even neo-fascist, for arguing for tough anti-fraud measures. But such vigilance is required if voters are to trust a political party with governance of the country in which £4 of every £10 spent by the government goes to welfare. While, thank God, Labour has begun to change its stance on countering fraud, the extent of fraud is not taken seriously enough by any political party.

A second factor, very important in the medium term, is the unsustainable increase for greater public spending as a percentage of total UK output for other public sector activies: increases in science and NHS budgets to protect us from future pandemics (Omicron is far from defeated); increase in social security; additional resources to transition to net-zero carbon by 2050; increases in defence expenditure in response to Russia and China (the military claim increasing it from 2 per cent of GDP to 3 per cent of GDP will just keep our military ability at the current level); and the need for more resources for education and levelling up.

As time goes on, there will be a growing backlash against a means-tested welfare provision that penalizes honesty and self-interest. This backlash will give the opportunity to campaign again on the strengths of an insurance-based welfare. The backlash against means testing will also be succoured by the reform of the National Insurance contributory system as it underpins the current reform of health and social care.

The crunch point to this particular aspect of the political debate will be seen through the prism of whether one is promoting a minimum income floor through National Insurance on which people can build by their own efforts without being penalized by loss of benefit. The alternative prism is a means-tested ceiling through which beneficiaries lose benefit as they build extra income through work and thereby lose means-tested assistance.

The word 'insurance' needs careful handling. Too often political antagonists have interpreted the word as one would in the private sector: building up a sum of money that will pay pensions or other benefits. That view should stand in stark contrast to my view of insurance, which envisages the building up of entitlement by paying monetary contributions and not by accruing a particular capital sum. This distinction will be crucial in those areas, such as financing of the NHS and social care, where the National Insurance debate will at some stage break loose from its present political ranking.

The coalition government put onto the statute book a new basic state pension which reduced the number of years of contributions that were required before a full state pension was earned. This reform is not sustainable in the long run. We will need to increase the number of contributary years in line with rising life expectancy. If the overall aim is to decrease means-tested welfare, the new state pension will need to have a value above Universal Credit. There will then remain, as there has been since the Beveridge Report, the issue of how rent is dealt with. Any realizable National Insurance reform will have to run alongside a system of housing benefit because National Insurance benefit will never be of high enough value to float everybody off means testing. Housing benefit reform will be a major reform in its own right.

The government's intention to fund health and social care reform from National Insurance contributions should be welcomed. Of course, the regressive nature of today's insurance system needs to be radically changed. Reformers need to campaign for making the insurance contribution progressive, to include all income and to tax the self-employed to a much greater extent. Self-employment rules in the current scheme lead to widespread full National Insurance contribution avoidance. Given the way inflation will result in payments into the insurance fund being devalued over time, these contributions need to be index-linked, as are certain government bonds.

Back to my view of self-interested altruism. It is here that National Insurance shows itself working with the grain of human interest. It is possible to develop further the extension of National Insurance cover. People will sign up to a contract from which they might not immediately benefit if they realize they will at some stage in their life make a claim on an entitlement for which they are paying. The more successful one is in advocating a form of contribution people can make, the greater the success will be in building up an alliance of popular support for extending insurance cover.

What part does National Insurance play in helping to make us more moral individuals? I have written that there's a limit to which most human beings support altruism in its purest form. But I've always believed that, through our support and development of a National Insurance scheme, we help to change the base side of our human nature. Because, if we may benefit some day, we're prepared to pay up front for the needs of people who are in immediate need. We've become better people as a result of this transaction, and reformers should make more of this in their advocacy. And the wider the National Insurance coverage, the greater will be the number of people who can't make contributions who are nevertheless granted benefit.

Aiming to work with the grain of human nature is the basis of countering the limits imposed by our being fallen creatures, yet created to be redeemed. Working with the grain of human nature is one way of explaining my advocacy of insurance over means-tested welfare. It is the DNA in the reform I advocated for the sale of council houses. It was back in 1975 that I gave the lecture entitled 'Do We Need Council Houses?' I gave two negative replies to the question.

The lesser reason I gave arose from looking at the national data on the proportion of income derived from council housing. It seemed to be in inexorable decline. I didn't believe this decline could be reversed without advocating a new contract by appealing to altruistic self-interest. Higher contributions might be forthcoming if we thereby allowed people to own their own home.

The reform also advocated that the increased revenue thereby gained was not there for mere statistical satisfaction but to be used to repair existing stock and, above all, build new accommodation. We all know what happened on that score.

But the reform was advocated on the basis again of working with the grain of human nature. Ownership also made a difference to how people treated the object in their care. People might do an endless amount of repairs if their housing was owned by themselves. More to the point, ownership saw many people embarking on massive improvements to their properties. Reform was also important for other political reasons: if wealth was more equitably redistributed, it would be a greater bulwark against despotism. I've always seen a spreading of the ownership of wealth as a very important cornerstone of democracy.

Likewise, my views on human nature have shaped my views on taxation. While I agree with Francis Bacon that wealth, like manure, can only do its job if it is spread around, I also believe there is a limit to how much taxation the public will allow.

If we look historically, it has been difficult for governments of any colour to maintain taxation as a share of national income above 33 to 34 per cent of GDP. (It has risen from 26.3 per cent in March 2021 to 32.7 per cent a year later.) One reason why I advocate the extension of a progressively based National Insurance system for financing health and social care is that, by advocating a system of mutuals to run health and welfare, this new deal would break the 33 to 34 per cent ceiling. (Even with the explosion of COVID-related expenditure, the Institute for Fiscal Studies (IFS) estimate the proportion will rise to 35 per cent.) For long-term financial security people would have to have, in effect, a new tax contract with which they were happy. The new pact might not last for eternity, but it would get us through many decades.

Likewise National Insurance linked to specific objectives helps keep down the standard rate of tax. I know hypothecation cannot reign everywhere, but I think the idea has more life in it than is presently assumed. Governments need, wherever possible, to reduce the standard rate of tax by finding an insurance base for other forms of necessary expenditure. Here is a danger, and I fully appreciate it: not to develop a rump end of expenditure covered by general taxation. But even here – if we take the police force, for example – people might be prepared to pay more if they saw a form of policing they supported more fully. A job of politicians in this instance would be to find ways of cross-subsidizing so that those poorer areas are not at a permanent disadvantage compared with richer areas if police expenditure is linked more directly to tax and contributions.

Here, then, is the basis of my Christian approach to politics. My vision has been dominated by my views on human nature. We are all fallen creatures, but open to be redeemed. One role of politicians is to offer programmes that achieve this objective. Another way of seeing this Christian cornerstone to politics is in the creation of programmes that work with, rather than against, this grain of human nature.

In these concluding paragraphs I have tried to set out the principles that have governed every day of my political life, from the first day stepping into CPAG in 1969 to the dictation of this concluding chapter of *Politics, Poverty and Belief.*

In Gratitude

Members of staff with whom I have worked closely have played an important part in the final manuscript of *Politics, Poverty and Belief: A Political Life*. Rhiannon Brace began to assemble the manuscript, and this task was worked on by Florence Gildea. Likewise with Andrew Forsey, who headed my parliamentary office, and who not only read through the manuscript but was a driver of all my parliamentary work. I comment in the text that I regard being able to work with Andrew as one of the providential blessings that have characterized my political life. My thanks are also due Joanna Moriarty, who read through the manuscript and suggested publishers. I am grateful too for the friendship and support Catherine and Johnny Armitage so fully give me; their generosity made it possible for me to work with Daniel Sanchez, without his help this book would not have been completed. I am also grateful to Matthew Taylor for his final work on the manuscript.

Last comes my biggest and most immediate thanks. I can say without hesitation that without Brian and Rachel Griffiths this book would never have appeared. Only I know how important their loving support has been in resisting the reserve I have felt writing about my views. In writing, I have realized that I separated the public side of my life, which I willingly undertook as an MP and which

I willingly accept is open to scrutiny, from my private beliefs. But the views that have inspired me and which, however inadequately, have given shape to my life, I have always been reticent to share.

Taking forward the ideas I have explained in *The Politics of Paradise* into a record of what I thought, rather than what others thought, has been an exercise that was more costly than I would have thought possible at the start of this endeavour. I hope the effort proves worthwhile to Brian and Rachel and, beyond them, to that part of the electorate to which I have always tried to appeal through my spoken and written word. It is this group which I have viewed as today's clerisy. It is they who, through their daily lives and actions, are entrusted with the defence of democratic freedom as we have come to know it. In return this group has shown a commitment to social justice that never fails to raise my spirits.

So, at last, I cast *Politics, Poverty and Belief* onto the waters and thereby hopefully into your hands, dear reader.

Frank Field
Westminster, October 2022

INDEX